New Creation Spirituality

New Creation Spirituality

Christianity in the 21st Century and Beyond

Michael Reinemann

New Creation Spirituality: Christianity in the 21st Century and Beyond
Copyright © 2020 Michael Reinemann

Scripture quotations marked (NIV) are taken from the New International Version®, NIV®. Copyright © 1973, 1978, 1984, 2011 by Biblica, Inc.™ Used by permission of Zondervan. All rights reserved worldwide. When not indicated, Scripture verses are NIV.

Scripture quotations marked (NASB) taken from the New American Standard Bible® (NASB), Copyright © 1960, 1962, 1963, 1968, 1971, 1972, 1973, 1975, 1977, 1995 by The Lockman Foundation. Used by permission.

Scripture quotations marked (NKJV) taken from the New King James Version®. Copyright © 1982 by Thomas Nelson. Used by permission. All rights reserved.

Scripture quotations marked (ESV) are from The ESV® Bible (The Holy Bible, English Standard Version®), copyright © 2001 by Crossway, a publishing ministry of Good News Publishers. Used by permission. All rights reserved.

Scriptures marked KJV are taken from the KING JAMES VERSION (KJV): KING JAMES VERSION, public domain.

ISBN: 978-1-7341594-2-4 (Paperback); 978-1-7341594-3-1 (E-book)

Italics or bold added in inset Scripture are the author's emphasis. Parenthetical annotations in Scripture passages are the author's. Scripture verses incorporated into the body text are italicized. Scriptures not otherwise designated are NIV.

Library of Congress Control Number: 2020907499

Cover artwork and design by Christa Walsh.

All rights reserved. No part of this publication may be reproduced, redistributed, or transmitted in any form or by any means, including photocopying, recording, or other electronic or mechanical methods, without the prior written permission of the publisher, except in the cases of brief quotations embodied in critical reviews and certain noncommercial uses permitted by copyright law.

Published in the United States of America.

SeekingHisMind Publications
www.seekingHismind.com

For the Body of Christ

"But an hour is coming, and now is, when the true worshipers will worship the Father in spirit and truth…" - John 4:23

"In Him we live and move and have our being." - Acts 17:28

Table of Contents

INTRODUCTION 13

CHAPTER ONE: A NEW REALITY 21
- THE ANOINTING 21
- THE NEW TEMPLE 27

PART ONE: PROPHETS 33

CHAPTER TWO: CARRIERS 35
- ETERNAL LIFE 37
- THE MIND OF CHRIST 42
- JESUS THE RABBI 44

CHAPTER THREE: IDENTIFIERS 49
- AS HE IS, SO ARE WE 51
- THE PROPHETIC BURDEN 55
- SIGNS AND SYMBOLS 57

CHAPTER FOUR: RELEASERS 63
- OPEN HEAVENS 68
- THE NATURE OF MIRACLES 71
- RELEASING THE WORD 76
- HEARING GOD'S VOICE 81
- RISK AND REWARD 84

PART TWO: PRIESTS 89

CHAPTER FIVE: THE ROYAL PRIESTHOOD 91
- OUR GREAT HIGH PRIEST 91
- LIVING STONES 94
- THE LAST ADAM AND THE NEW JERUSALEM 95

CHAPTER SIX: TRUE CHRISTIAN WORSHIP 101

Spirit and Truth	103
Cleaning House	104
Fruits of Worship	108
Prayer Without Ceasing	111

CHAPTER SEVEN: IT'S ALL IN THE FAMILY 115

Father Abraham Had Many Sons	116
Bread and Wine	120
The Dust of the Earth	126

CHAPTER EIGHT: THE GOOD NEWS COURIERS 131

The Master Evangelist	134
Tongues of Fire	137
If We Build It, They Will Come	142

PART THREE: KINGS 147

CHAPTER NINE: A NEW KIND OF KING 149

All Hail King Jesus	149
Servant Kings	153
Christ's Triumphal Procession	156
A Lesson from Corinth	158

CHAPTER TEN: THIS MEANS WAR 163

Principalities and Powers	164
Demolishing Strongholds and Killing Giants	166
Revelation's Seven Promises	171

CHAPTER ELEVEN: JUDGMENT DAY 179

The Cross is the Judgment	181
A Consuming Fire	183
Joel's Army	186

CHAPTER 12: THE SHAPE OF THINGS TO COME 193

The End is Near?	194

Honor Thy Father and Mother	198
New Perspectives	201
Iron Sharpens Iron	204

AUTHOR'S NOTE **209**

Introduction

Around two thousand years ago, the most significant series of events in human history occurred. A man named Jesus Christ gathered disciples, began a public ministry, faced cruel opposition, hung on a cross, died, and resurrected three days later. Fast forward twenty centuries and billions of people now call on Him as God. Who is this Jesus? Why is His message so powerful? How could one man possibly change the entire world?

Such questions preoccupy the minds of the world's spiritual seekers, Christians and non-Christians alike. They have certainly assumed a prominent position within my own consciousness. I feel these questions are like arterial roads that eventually collide at a major junction. This junction is the question of all questions, the one that is paramount in the Christian faith: what exactly was Jesus Christ doing on the cross?

The answer to this is more important than we may realize. Depending on who you ask and in what era of church history you are asking, you may hear wildly different answers. A first-century Messianic Jew would have very different ideas about the cross than a sixteenth-century Lutheran. The opinion of a twenty-first century Pentecostal would certainly contrast with that of an eighth-century Catholic. But, in your inquiry, you would undoubtedly discern some common terms and themes: sacrifice, sin, salvation, judgment, repentance, redemption, eternal life… the list goes on. However, you would discover that these terms actually mean different things to different people in different time periods. This can only lead to more questions. So, what is *most* correct and true? What does God actually want us to believe?

In matters of religion, are the blind leading the blind? As humans, we tend to just trust the people who are teaching us, assuming that they know what they are talking about. We put our faith in imperfect humans to guide and lead us into the truths of the scriptures. We figure that if a person is in some sort of position of authority, they must be correct and have our best interests in mind. Therefore, we trust them and their leadership implicitly. We go on like this for years, trusting others to lead and guide us into God's truth.

Now, what would happen if something you had learned to believe about God actually wasn't true? Not false, *per se*, but not true in the sense that it wasn't the *fullest* version of truth? What if there was an entirely new set of ideas concerning God, the Bible, and the Church that you had previously never encountered? How would you respond? Certainly, there would be some sort of torment of conscience, anxiety, questioning, maybe even anger. But what would happen if you put these new ideas to the test in your experience and realized they could provide you with greater spiritual freedom, an earnest love for others, a deeper relationship with Christ, a brighter outlook on life, and tangible experiences of the Holy Spirit? You would undoubtedly begin to think twice about the long-standing beliefs and set-in-stone ideas about God you had once considered unshakable.

This scenario is exactly what we witness happening today in the Church. There is an emergence of fresh new ideas about God and "His book," the Bible. Brave men and women, disappointed with the status quo of the faith today, are beginning to pioneer new understandings and fresh ways of thinking. Anyone aware of the Christian headlines will tell you that these new ways of thinking are producing some interesting results - rumors of spiritual awakening, widespread revival, and miracles sweep across the globe. In other words, there seems to be tangible fruit.

It is in this context that this book finds its home. This work is a response to the age we live in, with all of its myriad uncertainties, crises, challenges, and complexities. It emerges from the heart of a man deeply concerned about humanity's spiritual and moral future, and the role Christianity is destined to play in this future. Its truths were born and bred in the fires of spiritual adversity and personal experience. It is a counter to the perceived spiritual darkness of our time and the apparent decline of Christianity in the developed world.

New Creation Spirituality: Christianity in the 21st Century and Beyond

It can be easy to think that Christians are in no way responsible for the current decline of the faith. After all, the times are dark, we are told, and Satan is on the move. Powerful supernatural forces align against us. Just look at our leaders, our entertainment, our materialism, and our technology. Being human, we like to place the blame for the decline of the faith on everything or everyone but ourselves. Perhaps we need to start taking responsibility for our situation and realize that *our beliefs and behaviors* may be the reason Christianity seems so ineffective and irrelevant in our postmodern world. Maybe Isaiah was right when he wrote, *"God's name is blasphemed among the unbelievers because of you"* (Isaiah 52:5). Maybe Christianity's decline is in some way *our fault.*

A careful examination of the New Testament lends some credibility to this idea. In the gospels, Jesus drew the crowds. Everywhere He went, people came to Him. Who were His enemies? Certainly not the crowds of the people. His enemies were those in the established religious institution who could not stand this strange teacher's new ideas, popularity and miracle-working power. How did they address this growing threat to the political-religious institution? They killed Him.

If we look at the ministry of the early apostles, particularly Paul, we can see that most of the Jesus movement's "enemies" were not unbelievers, but the Jewish leaders. These men were so attached to their traditions and the self-righteous identity they found in their religion that the persecution of Paul became their life's mission. Like Jesus before him, most of Paul's issues came from the clash of the religious institution with the living Gospel. Paul became so fed up with this behavior from the Jewish people that he completely changed the direction of his ministry![1] Sure, there would be some hiccups and push-back from the Gentiles (non-Jews), but not as much as what came from the Jews.

You can see shadows of this pattern today in the Body of Christ because we have permitted and fostered sinful division. Religionism clashes against the newness and freedom that the Holy Spirit is trying to bring. Rife with our own internal problems, we have projected an undesirable image of Christ into the world. We tear and claw at each other over ideas, words, and

---

[1] See Luke's account in Acts 18.

doctrines. We slander each other endlessly and hold conferences to tear down those who think differently. It's embarrassing. Many unbelievers looking in from the outside want nothing to do with this "Christianity." As we self-implode, the train of the world's spiritual seekers passes right on by to neo-paganism, agnosticism, or atheism.

Clearly, there is a disconnect between the Church of the first century and the Church of today. What was once a thriving, vibrant spiritual movement that spread like wildfire and turned the world upside down has become a philosophical system that many roll their eyes at. What happened? What are we doing wrong?

I think perhaps Mahatma Gandhi put it best when he said, "I like your Christ, I do not like your Christians. Your Christians are so unlike your Christ." I believe Gandhi was right. Over the centuries, Christianity has lost its focus as a Spirit-empowered, social-spiritual movement and become a set of conceptual ideas designed to make us feel good about our relationship with God. The presence of God, genuine concern for our neighbor, and loving devotion to the Lord have been replaced with Sunday School, a dominating spiritual indifference, and a superficial, slavish religiosity. *"These people come near to me with their words, but their hearts are far from me,"* God tells the prophet Isaiah concerning ancient Israel (Isaiah 29:13). These words speak directly to the heart of our modern spiritual identity crisis. We are all head, no heart - all form, but no power. And, as we can see, we are currently eating the bitter fruits of this powerless faith.

Does God have a solution? I believe so, but I cannot claim to have all the answers. This book is my earnest desire to outline a new *way* to think, not *what* to think. New creation spirituality is not a new religion or a new Christian sect. It is not against the Church, but for Her. What I aim to do is capture the essence of the first-century Jesus movement and repackage it for the times we live in. I want to pour a timeless, ageless wine into a new bottle that we can firmly grasp and drink from. I desire to ignite people with faith, hope, and love - three essential ingredients for victorious Christian living. My primary concern is to answer this question: *How do God's people embody and manifest the fullness of Jesus Christ's victory on the cross*? This book explores this question.

"New Creation Spirituality." What's with that? In 2 Corinthians 5:17, Paul tells the believers that in Christ they have become an entirely "new creation." *"The old has come, the new is here!"* Paul triumphantly writes. This single verse contains in condensed form the worldview and perspective of the early church. The life, death, and resurrection of Jesus Christ overhauled the fabric of existence itself. Through the work of Christ and the subsequent sending of the Holy Spirit, God began His mission to redeem and heal the entire universe from sin's infection. The most amazing thing about this is the reality that God's glorious, all-encompassing redemption begins with humanity - you and me! The scriptures tell us that we are the "firstfruits" - the first manifest evidence - of a universe free from the grip of sin! This book is a journey into this vibrant new way of being, this new type of humanity. We will explore the worldview of the apostles, but in a way that is fresh and relevant for the times we live in.

I like the word "spirituality" because it lacks legalistic religious connotations. Those hurt or damaged by the modern Church may find resonance with this term. I meet many people who tell me, "I believe in Jesus Christ but not organized religion." I used to scoff at these people, but I now understand that underneath these words there is usually a church-based wound or a pain that was never able to heal properly. These believers love Jesus Christ just as much as anyone else, but, for one reason or another, the Church has driven them away. Although wary of the trappings of organized religion, they actively seek a deeper spiritual connection with God. I have found that many of these men and women have unique experiences with God or uncommon understandings that cause unease in the average churchgoer. Rather than seeking to bridge the divide in order to arrive at a mutual understanding, the Church ignores these people or pushes them out. It is no wonder they cannot imagine themselves inside of a church ever again.

Of course, we need each other, and I try to outline in this book a "spirituality" that promotes unity in diversity as well as a vibrant individual pursuit of God. The word "spirituality" at its core implies individualism. Ultimately, we alone are responsible for the development of our relationship with God and what we do with the gifts and graces that flow through us. The spiritual path into God's heart requires effort, not apathy. We are all called to contribute to what God is doing on Planet Earth, to act as a spiritual body with many parts. How can we do this effectively if individuals fail to take responsibility for their own growth? How can we feast at God's table if members of His family don't do their part in preparing the meal? We can't. We must learn how to become self-empowered, self-motivated members of God's royal family. This begins with rewiring the way we think about the faith.

I can sum up new creation spirituality with an analogy. Imagine your father is the richest man in the world. This man is not only fabulously wealthy, but full of love and care. For your birthday, he decides to buy for you the car of your dreams. What will you do when he rolls the car into the driveway for you to enjoy? Are you going to sit there and stare? Or will you get in the car and actually *drive it*.

This is a perfect analogy for Christianity today. The car is the resurrection life and the Father is none other than God Himself. Religion sits, stares, and explains, afraid to actually get in the car and drive, apprehensive of how God might respond. New creation spirituality gets in the car and drives with boldness and confidence.

The following chapters will require an open mind and heart. We will examine biblical truths from new angles you have perhaps never considered. Your religion, your set-in-stone conceptual beliefs about Jesus and His work on Earth, will be shaken. You will perhaps experience offense and wonder (as I often hear), "If this is true, why haven't I heard this before?" You will re-evaluate long-standing beliefs about God, His kingdom, and His purpose for your life.

Like a swig of strong alcohol, the presentation of genuine truth always provokes a visceral reaction. Examining our own false beliefs about God takes courage and not all can handle it. It can arouse fear, pride, and attacks from religionists and others zealously addicted to intellectual Christian dogma. Religion instills the belief that if we "believe" the wrong conceptual idea about God, He will hate us, and we will go to hell.

I find that many religionists cling (willfully or ignorantly) to an incomplete understanding of the gospel. The "gospel" that they believe in is not the first-century gospel of Jesus Christ, but a modified message heavily influenced by the Christianity of the dark ages and the theological insights of the Protestant Reformation. We have been duped into thinking that the "gospel" taught today in many modern Protestant and non-denominational churches was the same gospel that Paul and the apostles preached. As we will soon discover, this is simply not true. It is impossible to understand the *real* gospel without the backdrop of first-century Judaism. I am not a professional historian, but I aim to align the truths of this book with the worldview of the first-century Jesus movement.

It would perhaps help to state what the gospel of Jesus Christ is *not*. Jesus Christ did not come to forgive sin simply so we could find ourselves in heaven instead of hell after we leave this earth. In this "gospel," obedience to God is mandatory, lest we face eternal fire and torment. Obey to "be saved." Disobey and, well...you know the rest. Life on earth is one big slog until we reach the finish line of death. We will then escape from our miserable, dark, sinful existence on earth and fly away into radiant glory.

This is a perversion of the first-century gospel, which has been warped by the complexities and challenges of Church history. The first-century gospel was not primarily concerned with what happened *when* you died, although this was part of it. The real gospel was and is in a single word *restoration*. The God of Israel had forgiven the sins of the people in and through Jesus Christ, in order to reopen mankind's access to the presence of God. Jesus inaugurated a spiritual kingdom that "cannot be shaken." The pouring out of the Holy Spirit was a sign that God's promise to heal, restore, and redeem the entire cosmos had begun. Death and its allies had objectively been conquered on the cross (*"Jesus disarmed spiritual principalities and powers, triumphing over them by the cross,"* Paul writes in Colossians 2:15).

Those in Christ now find themselves in union with God, co-laboring with Him to hasten the fullness of the new creation. The restoration and renewal of the entire creation begins and ends with the Body of Christ, God's new humanity. The Body of Christ on earth is the visible representation of the ascended Jesus. We are in Him, and He is in us. *As He is, so are we in this world* (1 John 4:17).

What's left is the subjective experience of the reality of the new creation - a progressive unveiling of the kingdom of heaven and the "appearing" of Jesus Christ. What is most shocking is that the manifestation of this kingdom flows through the Body of Christ, God's overhauled new humanity. The restoration of creation has begun in humans, in order to be brought into full effect *through* humans.

These incredible realities serve as the platform for new creation spirituality, which we will soon begin to explore. It is my hope that this book will inspire you to think about God in new and exciting ways. By breathing fresh life into timeless scriptural truths, we will awaken to the fullness of who we are in Christ and inspire vision for the future. When we receive vision, we become divinely energized. When we become divinely energized, we become the men and women God intends us to be. When we become the men and women God intends us to be, we change the world.

Chapter One

A New Reality

Understanding new creation spirituality requires that we first grasp the biblical concept of the anointing. Comprehending the anointing is foundational for living as Spirit-empowered members of God's new humanity. The anointing is an essential element of our spiritual inheritance that Jesus Christ has freely given to us. It bestows upon every believer the spiritual roles of prophet, priest, and king in the current rule and reign of Christ. As we learn to live and mature into these roles, we experience the manifestation of God's heavenly kingdom.

The Anointing

A good way to gain deeper insight into New Testament kingdom realities is to examine the appropriate antecedents (preceding symbols) in the Old Testament. The Old Testament is full of thematic patterns, archetypes, and allusions that prepared Israel's heart for the greatest revelation of God: Jesus Christ. An Old Testament antecedent will use physical or natural principles to foreshadow spiritual realities in the kingdom of God.

The concept of New Covenant spiritual anointing is not without Old Testament precedent. In the Old Testament, the anointing was a smearing with sacred oil that symbolically inaugurated an individual into a special theocratic office. Israel's anointed individuals included prophets, priests, and kings. Some examples from Scripture now follow.

Saul's call to be the first king of Israel included an anointing from the prophet Samuel:

> "And Samuel took a vial of oil, and poured it on [Saul's] head, and kissed him, and said to him, 'Has not the Lord anointed thee for a ruler of his people, over Israel? And thou shalt rule among the people of the Lord, and thou shalt save them out of the hand of their enemies; and this shall be the sign to thee that the Lord has anointed thee for a ruler over his inheritance.'" 1 Samuel 10:1 (LXX)

Notice the emphasis in the above passage on inheritance, kingdom reign, and deliverance from enemies. These are all important themes that are explored in this book. The anointing leaves Saul a changed man – the ceremony is soon followed by a powerful and transformative prophecy session initiated by the Holy Spirit:

> "'The Spirit of the Lord will come powerfully upon you, and you will prophesy with them; and you will be changed into a different person'… As Saul turned to leave Samuel, God changed Saul's heart, and all these signs were fulfilled in that day. When he and his servant arrived at Gibeah, a procession of prophets met him; the Spirit of God came powerfully upon him, and he joined in their prophesying." 1 Samuel 10:6, 9-10 (NKJV)

This episode of Saul and the travelling prophets shows us that the Holy Spirit confirmed Saul's anointing with a visible demonstration of God's power. We can see that the anointing changed Saul into a completely different kind of person. Overshadowed by the Spirit of God, he became empowered and energized for his new role as Israel's king.

Israel's priests were anointed. During Moses' encounter with God on Mount Sinai, he received instructions for the construction of the tabernacle and the inception of the priesthood. Included in God's instructions to Moses is a directive to "anoint" those who would be priests in the tabernacle. These men would perform ritual service before the Lord.

> "So you [Moses] shall put them on Aaron your brother and on his sons with him. **You shall anoint them**, consecrate them, and sanctify them, **that they may minister to Me as priests.**" Exodus 28:41 (NKJV)

The anointing in this passage from Exodus has both a consecrating (setting apart) and sanctifying (purifying) function. This anointing prepared the priests for duty and worship in the tabernacle, the place of God's manifest presence amongst the people. During this meeting, God also told Moses that this priesthood will be perpetual - without end! We are the living fulfillment of these words. We perform priestly duties to the Lord in a spiritual manner.

Kings and priests were anointed, but so were prophets! A standout example from the Old Testament is Elisha, the successor of the prophet Elijah. After Elijah flees into the desert to escape the evil queen Jezebel, God consoles and encourages him on Mount Sinai. God then instructs Elijah to anoint Elisha, his prophetic successor.

> "Then the Lord said to him: 'Go, return on your way to the Wilderness of Damascus; and when you arrive, anoint Hazael as king over Syria. Also, you shall anoint Jehu the son of Nimshi as king over Israel. **And Elisha the son of Shaphat of Abel Meholah you shall anoint as prophet in your place**.'" 1 Kings 19:15-16 (NKJV)

From these passages, we can glean the symbolic purpose of the anointing. This was God's way of commissioning individuals for the role of king, priest, or prophet. An anointing indicated God's approval of individuals for these roles. The men in these offices were considered to have no earthly superior and answered directly to God.

We now turn to Jesus Christ. The word "Christ" in the Greek is *christos,* which means "anointed." Although anointed individuals ("christs" = anointed ones) had preceded Him in Israel's theocratic structure, Jesus was *the* Christ. He was the fulfillment of the prophetic promises God had been making to humanity since the time of Abraham. God's covenant people, the Jews, bound by oppression for centuries, were eagerly awaiting a dramatic overthrow of the Roman government and the installation of a tangible Messianic kingdom. Instead, Jesus revealed and initiated a different *kind* of kingdom on earth. Something shockingly cosmic and universal had taken place on the cross: Jesus Christ overhauled the very nature of humanity through His life, death, and resurrection. Christ has raised mankind to new life and has brought us into His kingdom.[2] In this kingdom, a new humanity brims with Christ's resurrection life through the anointing of the Holy Spirit. The anointing, which had once been a symbolic religious gesture, is now *spiritually* realized amongst New Covenant believers!

Both Paul and John tap into this understanding of our spiritual anointing in their writings.

In Paul:

> "Now He who establishes us with you in Christ and has anointed us is God, who also has sealed us and given us the Spirit in our hearts as a guarantee." 2 Corinthians 1:21-22 (NKJV)

In John:

> "But you have an anointing from the Holy One, and you know all things." 1 John 2:20 (NKJV)

> "But the anointing which you received from Him abides in you, and you do not need anyone to teach you; but as the same anointing teaches you concerning all things, and is true, and is not a lie, and just as it has taught you, you will abide in Him." 1 John 2:27 (NKJV)

The apostles understood that the act of anointing in Israel's history foreshadowed the unlimited anointing of the Holy Spirit given to mankind

---

[2] "You were buried with him in baptism, and were also raised with him through your faith in the working of God, who raised him from the dead." Colossians 2:12 (NIV)

by God through Christ. This new anointing empowers the Church for service in Christ's kingdom reign, which has already begun. The early church's evangelistic concern was spreading the message of mankind's restored relationship with God and inclusion in His kingdom reign. *"He has rescued us from the dominion of darkness,"* Paul writes, *"and has brought us into the kingdom of the Son He loves, in whom we have redemption (restoration), the forgiveness of sins"* (Colossians 1:13-14, NIV). The anointing is what empowers the Church to manifest Christ's character, love, and power. The forgiveness of sin is what makes this possible.

A Christian or "Christ one" (again, Christ means anointed) is not someone who simply follows the teachings and maxims of Jesus or strives to intellectually align themselves with one type of religious dogma over another. Before Christianity hardened into a formalized religious structure, it was a lifestyle, a *modus operandi*. It was a *way of being*. A Christian is someone who shares in the anointing of the Holy Spirit in order to join Christ in bringing about the manifestation and fullness of His kingdom. Because Jesus completely restored mankind's connection with the Father on the cross, every man and woman now has the ability to walk in and personally experience the anointing of the Holy Spirit and, thus, friendship and intimacy with the living God. We are ultimately answerable to God alone for our identity, thoughts, behaviors, and lifestyle. When we finally meet Jesus in person, we will be held accountable for how we stewarded His anointing.

The anointing propels us into the spiritual roles of prophets, priests, and kings in God's advancing kingdom. These roles allow us to live spiritually-empowered lifestyles that radiate the light and love of Christ into a dark and unbelieving world. Understanding the roles and responsibilities of the kingdom prophet, priest, and king is essential for living out the truths of the Christian faith in the 21st century and beyond. They are the pillars of new creation spirituality.

1. We are a prophetic people. We share the vision and heart of our heavenly Father. We are able to hear from God directly and declare His truths. Like Jesus, we live to say what the Father is saying and do what the Father is doing. We experience subjective revelation, which enhances our understanding of the objective truths found in the scriptures. God communicates with us directly through the mind. We are living signs and symbols of what God is saying and doing in the heavenly realm.

2. We are a priestly people. We host, reflect, and manifest the very presence of God. The new humanity is the location of God's revelatory presence on earth. As we abide in holiness and purity and offer our bodies as living sacrifices, God manifests Himself in and through us. We offer priestly sacrifices to God through prayer, worship, fellowship, and evangelism.

3. We are a royal people. We share in the current rule and reign of Jesus Christ. Made in the image of God, we represent God's divine likeness. Our suffering alongside the risen Christ ushers in His glory and manifests His kingdom. We will judge the world with Jesus.

This book is based on the simple premise that all believers are called to operate in these three roles simultaneously. Fully understanding these roles allows us to more effectively operate in our mandate to be God's "ministers of reconciliation."[3] Our mission is to draw a lost world back into the arms of a loving Father. The anointing of the Holy Spirit is what ultimately makes this possible.

Today, the Lord is breaking the Church out of her religious boxes and formalized structures. It is not that these things are inherently bad or evil, of course. In fact, tradition is the primary reason the Church is still alive twenty centuries after its inception. However, when tradition fails in its primary purpose - to act as a catalyst for Spirit-empowered daily living, genuine worship of the living God, and deep concern for humanity - it becomes cold and lifeless. The Holy Spirit is returning the Church to its roots as a social-spiritual movement, where conscious awareness of God's presence saturates and pervades every area of life.

It is so important to understand that this anointing is not an *it*, but the person of the Holy Spirit, who now imbues our humanity with the energies of Christ. Through the Holy Spirit, the "born again" humanity partakes and participates in the divine nature of Christ. This empowers us for a life of

---

[3] "God was reconciling the world to himself in Christ, not counting people's sins against them. And he has committed to us the message of reconciliation. We are therefore Christ's ambassadors..." 2 Corinthians 5:19-20 (NIV)

faithfulness and service to God. The apostle Peter writes the following about the divine nature:

> "His divine power has given us everything we need for a godly life through our knowledge of him who called us by his own glory and goodness. Through these he has given us his very great and precious promises, so that through them you may participate in the divine nature, having escaped the corruption in the world caused by evil desires." 2 Peter 1:3-4 (NIV)

The anointing is the *divine nature*, which radiates through our humanity so that we may manifest Christ and continue His mission to restore the entire cosmos. It completely frees us from the vices and sinful bondages that belong to the old creation order. In our human weakness, we are made strong through the anointing, the divine energies of Christ that flow through us and testify to the reality of the new creation. *"We have this treasure* (the divine nature of Christ) *in jars of clay* (imperfect humanity),*"* Paul writes, *"to show that this all-surpassing power is from God and not from us. We are hard pressed on every side, but not crushed; perplexed, but not in despair; persecuted, but not abandoned; struck down, but not destroyed. We always carry around in our body the death of Jesus, so that the life of Jesus may also be revealed in our body"* (2 Corinthians 4:7-10, NIV). The "life of Jesus" in this passage is the breaking in of the reality of the new creation order, which has already begun to eclipse the brokenness, sin, and decay of the old-world order that is passing away.

The New Temple

The anointing testifies of another astonishing spiritual reality: The Body of Christ is the new temple of the living God. This is another key reality that must be comprehended in order for us to live in the fullness of our new creation destiny and calling. It informs and empowers our roles as prophets, priests, and kings in the new creation. Before we can investigate these new creation pillars, we must understand their foundation - the new temple.

"Temple" is a loaded term for the Jewish people. For a first-century Jew (and the Hebrew people before), the temple was the center of all life. It was the place where God came from heaven to dwell and inhabit. It was the location of heaven meeting earth. In other words, it was the place of union between the divine and human. It was a kind of interdimensional rift (think sci-fi movies here) where spiritual acts of worship would cause God's realm ("heaven") to break into the human realm ("earth"). The temple was an extremely special place that lay at the heart of Israel's worship of God.

There is a kind of temple theme or motif that runs through Scripture. There are different locations in the Bible that are understood to be the place of God's manifest personal presence. Although we know God is everywhere[4], there are specific places of *revelatory* presence - where God becomes tangible, manifest, and obvious to the human senses. Prominent examples of the temple motif in the Bible are the garden of Eden, where God walked with Adam and Eve, Mount Sinai, where God appeared to Moses and Elijah, the wilderness tabernacle, and Solomon's temple. Associated with these places are all sorts of terrific "supernatural" events - rushing winds, flaming fire, earthquakes, glory so heavy priests cannot stand, etc. The point is that the temple is a place where natural reality synergizes with God's reality.

It will help us to stop thinking of heaven as a fixed location. Think instead of heaven as God's realm (Hebrew: *shamayim*, Greek: *ouranos*), which transcends time, space, and matter. Heaven is a place, yes, but we tend to oversimplify it as some sort of distant locale beyond the stars, a home for saintly spirits, far removed from human existence and comprehension. The early Christians, however, would have understood "heaven" as God's reality, God's *realm of being*. It is not confined to a time or place. Thus, the Holy Spirit is God's heavenly agent who "manifests" God's reality into human reality. We do not need to "call down" heaven or work our way into it - the Holy Spirit is the manifestation of heaven and God's kingdom. When the ancient Israelites experienced "glory" on Mount Sinai or in the temple, it was a *manifestation* of the reality of God's realm.

Six hundred years before Christ, when the Israelites were hopelessly exiled into Babylon, the prophets gazed into the future and envisioned a kind of new temple that would supersede all others. In this new temple, God would return and make His presence obvious and evident to all men. Glory, or manifest

---

[4] "Where can I go from your Spirit? Where can I flee from your presence? If I go up to the heavens, you are there; if I make my bed in the depths, you are there." Psalm 139:7-8 (NIV)

presence, would return to Zion, the prophets promised. As a result, the nations would stream to the new temple to learn about God and walk in His ways. It was just a matter of *when*.

Now fast forward past the prophets a few hundred years and Jesus rolls onto the scene of public ministry. He enters the temple complex in Jerusalem, throws over some tables, and drives the money changers and corrupt traders out with a whip. The Jews ask Him, *"What sign do you show to us, since you do these things?"* Jesus enigmatically replies with, *"Destroy this temple and in three days I will raise it up"* (John 2:19, NIV). The Jews and the disciples thought He was talking about the physical temple. No one had any idea what Jesus was actually talking about...until the resurrection and the giving of the Holy Spirit.

Jesus was, in essence, claiming Himself to be the new temple, the new place of Israel's worship of the living God. How is this possible? Remember, Jesus is the incarnate God. He is God's reality ("heaven!") meeting human reality as the divine nature and the human nature spin together in a synergistic fusion - a union. Jesus embodies the totality of the presence of God.

In the letter to the Colossians, Paul comments on this truth, writing:

> "The Son is the image of the invisible God, the firstborn over all creation. For in him all things were created: things in heaven and on earth, visible and invisible, whether thrones or powers or rulers or authorities; all things have been created through him and for him. He is before all things, and in him all things hold together...For God was pleased to have all his fullness dwell in him, and through him to reconcile to himself all things, whether things on earth or things in heaven, by making peace through his blood, shed on the cross." Colossians 1:15-20 (NIV)

In this passage, there is clear "heaven and earth" language. Jesus, as fully divine and fully human, is the new singularity, the new meeting point of the two realms. "He is before all things visible and invisible," Paul writes, "and in Him these invisible and visible things are held together." Jesus Christ is the new location of God's reality and manifest presence.

As members of the new creation, we are invited to participate in this new temple reality. The Bible says over and over again that the new humanity, the Body of Christ, are "in Christ." We should understand this quite literally. Jesus, who has "ascended" into God's realm and now fills the entire universe, is like a spiritual vortex. He pulls us into participating in what Paul calls the "fullness": *"For in Christ all the fullness of the Deity lives in bodily form,"* Paul states, *"and in Christ you have been brought into the fullness"* (Colossians 2:9-10, NIV). The fullness is God's reality, the Son holding power over all things seen and unseen and dispensing His authority to His prophets, priests, and kings as He deems necessary.[5] In this fullness, God's realm collides with our realm. The reality of the new creation, the manifestation of heaven, breaks in.

This reality is enabled and empowered by the anointing, the person of the Holy Spirit, who lives within us both as individuals and as a corporate spiritual body. Paul writes to the believers in Corinth: *"Do you not know that you are the temple of God and that the Spirit of God dwells in you?"* (1 Corinthians 3:16, NIV). Peter writes: *"You also, as living stones, are being built up as a spiritual house, a holy priesthood, to offer up spiritual sacrifices acceptable to God through Jesus Christ"* (1 Peter 2:5, NIV). In Revelation, the apostle John hears a loud voice from heaven that proclaims: *"Behold the tabernacle (temple) of God is with men, and He will dwell with them, and they shall be His people"* (Revelation 21:3, NIV).

As God's anointed people, the Church is much more than its buildings, dogmas, and intellectual precepts. We are a new humanity that carries God's glorious presence and lives to manifest His love and power. We are the temple of God, the place in which heavenly glory penetrates and permeates the earthly sphere of existence. He has chosen us to expand the awareness of His presence and glory. As we become the people He has called us to be and reveal the gospel (the real gospel), sin's power is broken and "territory" is taken for God's spiritual kingdom. Our mission on earth is God's desire - that all nations come to realize their glorious inheritance in Christ Jesus and experience the fullness of His eternal life.

---

[5] "Then Jesus came to them and said, 'All authority in heaven and on earth has been given to me. Therefore go and make disciples of all nations, baptizing them in the name of the Father and of the Son and of the Holy Spirit.'" Matthew 28:18 (NIV)

The realities of the anointing and the new temple lay the basic framework for our deeper exploration of new creation spirituality. They are the engine that powers the spiritual offices of prophet, priest and king. My goal in the following pages is to outline a way of thinking about God and the Bible that empowers us to become self-driven and passionate anointed ones, full of energy, purpose, and vision. We will learn to embody a new spirituality and an entirely new way of being. By exploring the anointed offices, we will step more completely into our divine sonship and, perhaps, catch a glimpse of the future of the faith.

Part One

Prophets

When you hear the word "prophet," what comes to mind? Is it a bearded old man with a flowing cloak and a long staff who is eager to impart his wisdom to impressionable young minds? Is it a raving madman who claims to hear from God? Perhaps an imagined picture of biblical prophets like Isaiah and Jeremiah comes to mind. Do you think of Jesus?

Today, there is a big misconception about prophets in the Body of Christ. For twenty years of living in the Christian faith, I had no idea that prophets could actually exist in today's day and age. If I came across anyone who claimed to be a prophet, I usually found them to be weird. My thinking changed when I later gained a deeper understanding of what exactly makes someone a "prophet."

We are all prophets in the currently advancing kingdom of God. God's Spirit-people, His anointed ones, are a *prophetic people*. We are prophetic in the sense that we have the ability to hear and respond to God's voice in order to manifest His will. Our access to the voice of the Father is made possible through the anointing, the person of the Holy Spirit. This access to God's presence and voice invite us to share in His reality (again, think "heaven").

I offer a simple definition of a modern Christian prophet:

A prophet is an anointed individual who carries, identifies with, and releases the presence of Jesus Christ.

The prophetic life is truly multi-layered and multi-faceted. At its core we find these three essential responsibilities: carry, identify with, release. We will examine each of these characteristics in turn.

Chapter Two

Carriers

Prophets carry the presence of Jesus Christ. The anointing plugs us into the heart and mind of God. Because of this, all believers constitute a *prophetic people*. We carry this connection to God's mind and heart with us wherever we go. We are each a type of miniature temple - walking and talking singularities where heaven and earth come into union.

As Christians, most of us have been taught that the Holy Spirit lives "within us" and that He "seals us for the day of redemption." These are wonderful truths of the faith but unless we fully grasp what they mean, they are just theological dogmas that make us feel good about ourselves. What does it mean to *carry* the very presence of God?

One of the most famous Bible verses of all time is Galatians 2:20. In it, Paul states that he died, and Jesus Christ now lives in him and through him:

> "I am crucified with Christ: nevertheless I live; yet not I, but Christ liveth in me: and the life which I now live in the flesh I live by the faith of the Son of God, who loved me, and gave himself for me." Galatians 2:20 (KJV)

Paul's perspective was that he had died on the cross with Jesus Christ because Jesus, as the Word of God, represented and embodied all of humanity (and humanity's sin) on the cross. In a spiritual, metaphysical sense, Paul hung on the cross with Christ and died with him (more on this later!). In this verse, Paul seems to claim that the ascended Jesus has assumed his body and is now using it to spread the message of heaven. Is this kind of creepy or do we just misunderstand?

It goes back to understanding the Jewish concept of life and death. Life to the Jews was God's personal presence. Death was rebellion and exile from God's presence because of willful sin. *"You were dead in your sins and transgressions,"* Paul writes in Ephesians 2:1. This word "dead" means completely devoid of God's presence and life. Sin had caused this "death"- perceived separation from God's presence. This death robbed mankind of our God-given humanity, so much so that we had begun to "regress" towards a purely animalistic nature, in order to gratify the desires of the flesh.[6] "Flesh" is the nature of humanity without Christ's empowering life. The mind governed by the flesh is death.[7]

But there is some great news (gospel) because of Christ! Let's examine the full passage from Ephesians 2 now.

> "As for you, you were dead in your transgressions and sins, in which you used to live when you followed the ways of this world and of the ruler of the kingdom of the air, the spirit who is now at work in those who are disobedient. All of us also lived among them at one time, gratifying the cravings of our flesh and following its desires and thoughts. Like the rest, we were by nature deserving of wrath. But because of his great love for us, God, who is rich in mercy, made us alive with Christ even when we were dead in transgressions - it is by grace you have been saved. And God raised us up with Christ and seated us with him in the heavenly realms

---

[6] "But these people blaspheme in matters they do not understand. They are like unreasoning animals, creatures of instinct, born only to be caught and destroyed, and like animals they too will perish." 2 Peter 2:12 (NIV)

"These people slander whatever they do not understand, and the very things they do understand by instinct – as irrational animals do – will destroy them." Jude 10 (NIV)

[7] "The mind governed by the flesh is death, but the mind governed by the Spirit is life and peace." Romans 8:6 (NIV)

in Christ Jesus, in order that in the coming ages he might show the incomparable riches of his grace, expressed in his kindness to us in Christ Jesus." Ephesians 2:1-7 (NIV)

We were once "dead" - devoid of God's presence - but God has now made us "alive." In fact, we are more than "alive," but seated with Christ in the heavenly realms. The Holy Spirit has breathed an entirely new kind of life into humanity. Our dry, dead bones, formerly full of rot, sin and decay have been overhauled and re-energized. We now brim with Christ-life, the anointing of the Holy Spirit. The old creation - subject to sin, decay, and death is gone - the new creation is here! Our separation and our autonomy from God have been done away with. We now live a new life that flows in the energizing presence of Jesus Christ. We were crucified with Him and He now lives within us.

To be "sealed with the Holy Spirit" is not a simple theological tidbit that makes us feel good enough to pass through the pearly gates of heaven when we die. It quite literally means that Christ's Spirit has assumed our body, mind, and heart to accomplish His mission on earth. This may initially come across as violating and offensive, but we are the ones who ultimately choose whether or not to submit to this new reality. Will we continue in our sin and death, or submit the totality of our being to a loving God who rules the universe?

Eternal Life

As God's prophetic people, we carry the life of Christ with us wherever we go. A commonly believed myth in modern Christianity is that the eternal life offered by Jesus Christ begins primarily after we leave this earth. Despite the prevalence of this understanding today, its theology is far removed from that of the Bible writers. We must, like them, understand that eternal life began the moment Jesus was resurrected.

The word "eternal" in the Bible is used both quantitatively and qualitatively. We tend to fixate on the quantitative definition of eternal life - life that goes on forever, *perpetual* life. We ignore the qualitative definition of eternal life: newness, fullness, wholeness, completion, empowerment, etc. "Eternal" describes a *quality* of life.

Throughout the New Testament, we should approach the word "eternal" mostly in a qualitative sense. The idea that the New Testament writers primarily intended "eternal life" to refer to some sort of veiled existence beyond the temporal was an idea developed centuries after Jesus Christ. The Bible writers were not fixated on escaping their present reality in order to find comfort and solace in the mysterious beyond. This idea is much more in line with the Buddhist concept of nirvana than it is with ancient Christianity. Rather, it was quite the opposite: the eternal, heavenly life of God had already begun to illuminate their reality. Jesus, the embodiment of the Father's eternal life, had assumed a human body to begin the mission of healing the entire creation order from sin's infection. The eternal life made available in Jesus allowed the early church to live victorious lives in the present, thanks to the empowering reality of the Holy Spirit. Hence, the apostle John writes about eternal life as a *present reality* for believers. Notice John's use of the present tense in the following passages:

In his gospel:

> "Whoever believes in the Son **has** eternal life, but whoever rejects the Son will not see life, for God's wrath remains on them." John 3:26 (NIV)

> "Very truly I (Jesus) tell you, whoever hears my word and believes him who has sent me **has eternal life** and will not be judged but **has crossed over from death to life**." John 5:24 (NIV)

> "Very truly I (Jesus) tell you, the one who believes **has eternal life**." John 6:47 (NIV)

In his first Epistle:

> "The life appeared; we have seen it and testify to it, and we proclaim to you the eternal life, which was with the Father and **has appeared to us**." 1 John 1:2 (NIV)

"And this is the testimony: **God has given us eternal life**, and this life is in his Son." 1 John 5:11 (NIV)

What is the core essence of "eternal life?" It is an intimate knowledge of the heavenly Father through an experience of Jesus Christ. The Lord Himself testified to this reality when He prayed to the Father, *"Now this is eternal life: that they know you, the only true God, and Jesus Christ, whom you have sent"* (John 17:3, NIV).

Eternal life is Jesus Himself, who has healed the separation between God and man. Through the cross, the Lord has restored humanity's ability to access and experience God's presence. For the Jewish people (i.e. the Bible writers), life *is* God's presence. To be absent from God's presence is to be living in death. Absence from God's presence prevents us from living in the fullest realization of our God-given design.

The rejection of God's presence is what had originally brought sin and death upon humanity. There was no sin and death before Adam and Eve's fall in the Garden of Eden. Sin and death entered the world after they attempted to seize autonomy from God. Christ, the last Adam, abolished this mistake of Adam and Eve. The cross completely destroyed the power of sin and death by restoring humanity's ability to access the presence of God.

The entire earth awaits the subjective experience of the cross' victory over sin and darkness. Day by day, we step further into the fullness of what Jesus has already accomplished on the cross. The Church is learning, growing, and maturing as a spiritual body. One day, humanity will no longer experience sin, decay, or death. Christ is presently at work in and through His people to hasten this Day, in which there will be a full union and unity between heaven and earth.[8]

Eternal life must be framed in the context of first-century Jewish socio-political expectation. The Jews, per the promises of their prophets, were awaiting a ruling king who would topple Roman oppression and establish the kingdom of God on earth. Crippled Israel, still in "exile" under Roman

---

[8] See 2 Peter 3:12 and Ephesians 1:10.

imperial rule and bound to a lifeless religious system, would be restored to its former glory as the leading nation on the earth...or so they had hoped.

Instead, Jesus Christ came with a spiritual mission. He came to heal spiritual death, which would in turn bring life in all areas - the physical, emotional, communal, etc. His life, crucifixion, and resurrection healed mankind's relationship with God, allowing us restored access to His presence. He healed the spiritual death of the Jewish people, whose relationship with the Father had long been overrun by religious pretense, ritual, and oppressive legalism. The coming of the Breath of God, the Holy Spirit, on both Jews and Gentiles was the fulfillment of God's promise to the prophet Ezekiel: the dry bones of Israel would rise and live again![9] Death, the consequence of mankind's sin, had been vanquished on the cross. Life abundant, enabled by restored access to the presence of God, has now become available. The kingdom of heaven has come near!

Eternal life, the present reality of heaven, is the core message of the gospel and what we embody as God's prophetic people. Paul writes about eternal life as an ever-increasing present reality, which will continue (not begin) in our life beyond this life:

> "He has saved us and called us to a holy life - not because of anything we have done but because of his own purpose and grace. This grace was given us in Christ Jesus before the beginning of time, but it has now been revealed through the appearing of our Savior, Christ Jesus, who has **destroyed death and has brought life and immortality to light** through the gospel." 2 Timothy 1:9-10 (NIV)

Life and immortality have been "brought to light through the gospel." Before, they were veiled, shadowy, and uncertain. Jesus Christ has now made them obvious – He has brought them to light. Eternal life is within God's prophetic people - it courses through our veins. It is the living water of the Holy Spirit, the anointing of Jesus Christ, who brings life and God's power to anything and everything we do.

---

[9] See Ezekiel 37:1-14.

> "Jesus answered, 'Everyone who drinks this water will be thirsty again, but whoever drinks the water I give them will never thirst. Indeed, the water I give them will become in them a spring of water welling up to eternal life.'" John 4:13-14 (NIV)

> "'Whoever believes in me (Jesus), as Scripture has said, rivers of living water will flow from within them.' By this he meant the Spirit, whom those who believed in him were later to receive…" John 7:38-39 (NIV)

In the above passages, Jesus alludes to the fact that the Holy Spirit is the fulfillment of Jewish prophecy concerning a living spiritual water that would come to flow in and through the people of God. Just look at some of the prophetic promises concerning this "living water":

In Isaiah:

> "With joy you will draw water from the wells of salvation." Isaiah 12:3 (NIV)

> "The lame will leap like a deer, and the mute tongue shout for joy. Water will gush forth in the wilderness and streams in the desert." Isaiah 35:6 (NIV)

> "For I will pour water on the thirsty land (Israel), and streams on the dry ground; I will pour out my Spirit on your offspring, and my blessing on your descendants. They will spring up like grass in a meadow, like poplars by flowing streams." Isaiah 44:3 (NIV)

And in Ezekiel:

> "Wherever the river flows, there will be swarms of living creatures and a great number of fish, because it flows there and makes the waters fresh; so wherever the river flows everything will flourish." Ezekiel 47:9 (NIV)

God's prophets carry this living water, this eternal life, which is wholeness and completion found only through the presence of God. His life is a current reality for all believers. It is an experience of God's glory that begins now and will continue forever. As God's prophets destined to carry His presence, we lay hold of this eternal life and allow His river of living water to flow freely in and through us.

The Mind of Christ

The reality of the indwelling Christ, with the fullness of His eternal life, is the empowering source of the prophetic lifestyle. We do life in tandem with Christ. He lives "within" in the sense that He enlightens and energizes every area of our humanity - mind, body, and spirit. It is not a mere conceptual reality. The Spirit of God who raised Jesus from the dead now lives within us and fills every area of our being with the Christ-life.[10] He walks with us, energizing us with His presence and heaven's eternal life.

The anointing enables the prophetic lifestyle, but it is the mind of Christ that activates it. I am so passionate about the mind of Christ's role in the new creation that I wrote an entire book about it. To avoid being redundant, I will summarize here only what is necessary to enhance our understanding of the prophetic function of the anointing.

Jesus, our model and pattern, lived a life flowing in the Holy Spirit. He was perfectly connected to God's mind. As such, He only did what He saw the Father doing and only said what He heard the Father saying.

> "Very truly I tell you, the Son can do nothing by himself; he can do only what he sees His Father doing, because whatever the Father does the Son also does." John 5:19 (NIV)

Through the gift of the Holy Spirit and the anointing, God has also given us the ability to live in the flow of the Father's voice. This allows us to live a "here as in heaven" lifestyle, a central theme of the Lord's Prayer. The idea

---

[10] "And if the Spirit of him who raised Jesus from the dead is living in you, he who raised Christ from the dead will also give life to your mortal bodies through his Spirit who lives in you." Romans 8:11 (NIV)

is that the character and nature of God's spiritual reality ("heaven") manifest and make themselves apparent in our realm ("earth"). The new humanity, the Body of Christ, is the conduit of the life of heaven and God's agent of change on earth.

We cannot enact the will of heaven without an awareness of what God is thinking and saying. This is where the mind of Christ comes in. The mind of Christ connects our human consciousness with the consciousness of God the Father. This allows us to live in an ever-increasing awareness of His will. If we can think like the Father, we can act like Jesus. God has freely given us the mind of His Son.

> "What we have received is not the spirit of the world, but the Spirit who is from God, so that we may understand what God has freely given us. This is what we speak, not with words taught us by human wisdom but in words taught by the Spirit, explaining spiritual realities with Spirit-taught words...we have the mind of Christ." 1 Corinthians 2:12-16 (NIV)

The mind of Christ plugs us into God's reality, His way of thinking. We can speak forth His "spiritual realities" with "Spirit-taught" words. This is a weighty responsibility for God's new humanity, and we must grow in learning how to steward it. Our words and actions carry weight, which is one reason why the apostles spend so much time in their letters addressing behavior. They understood themselves to be God's representatives to a lost humanity in desperate need of the Father's love. *"If anyone should speak,"* Peter warns, *"they should do so as one who speaks the very words of God"* (1 Peter 4:11, NIV).

God's prophetic people are called to live in tune with the divine will. Our ability to discern the voice of the Father requires time and spiritual practice (worship, prayer, reading the scriptures, etc.). As we grow in Christ, we increase our ability to flow in the Holy Spirit and live in an awareness of what the Father is doing and saying. Our eyes also open to the fact that we do not need to do anything to "earn" more of God's presence, because we already have all of Him living within us. Seated with Christ in heavenly places, we have been brought into God's fullness. As God's anointed ones and His new temple, we have been gifted His presence to steward. Our desire to please the

Lord flows from this simple reality. We act as God's children not because we have to, but because we *want* to. He walks with us! As we steward this remarkable reality, the Holy Spirit enlightens our hearts and minds to the totality of what has already been made available in Christ.

Jesus the Rabbi

A truth of Christian spirituality that is easy to believe but sometimes harder to experience is the reality that we are never alone. We walk with the ascended Christ through the Holy Spirit. We share Christ's mind and He teaches us to walk in the ways of God's truth. We learn to think and act as righteous sons and daughters.

God's prophets allow themselves to be taught and instructed by the Holy Spirit. This is an essential responsibility of carrying the anointing. John the apostle writes that we *"have an anointing from the Holy One, and we know all things"* and *"the anointing we have received from God remains in us, teaching us about all things. It is not counterfeit, but real, and we are called to abide in it"* (1 John 2:20,27, NIV).

John mentions that the anointing teaches us "about all things." These "things" are not just biblical truths, but moment-to-moment guidance on how to navigate a warped and crooked world that has fallen away from God. God desires His presence to saturate every area of our lives. The anointing empowers us to live in the ways of the kingdom and protects us from deception and the lies of our spiritual enemies.

The Bible indicates that ancient Christianity began as an intuitive (not intellectual) faith and spirituality. It was about the emergence of a new, overhauled inner world that radiates with the light and clarity of Jesus Christ, whose presence taught the disciples and apostles how to escape and live above the corruption of the "present evil age."[11] The ancient faith was less concerned with intellectual knowledge about God, and more concerned with living as Christ's newly formed, Spirit-empowered family. The kingdom of God is not a matter of talk, but a matter of manifesting the intent of God.[12]

---

[11] "He gave himself for our sins to rescue us from the present evil age." Galatians 1:4 (NIV)

[12] "For the kingdom of God is not a matter of talk but of power." 1 Corinthians 4:20 (NIV)

Intellectual truths, doctrines, dogmas, and theologies of the faith obviously have their place, but their ultimate purpose is to launch us into a new spiritual reality. In the New Covenant, the Holy Spirit is our primary teacher. As we actively abide in Him, He empowers us to walk in His ways. These "ways" are not mere religious obedience, but a lifestyle that bursts with the resurrection life of Christ. John writes, *"the one who abides in Him must also walk in the same manner as He* (Christ) *walked"* (1 John 2:6, NIV). And what is the manner in which Christ walked? It was total obedience to the spontaneous will of the Father and complete submission to the empowering presence of the Holy Spirit. Jesus Himself said, *"I have come down from heaven not to do my will but to do the will of him who sent me"* (John 6:36, NIV).

God's prophetic people live in a state of perpetual spiritual growth. We allow ourselves to be continually taught by the Spirit, who uses every life experience to shape our understanding and awareness of heaven's reality. *"Blessed are the poor in spirit,"* Jesus said, *"for theirs is the kingdom of heaven"* (Matthew 5:3, NIV). To be "poor in spirit" is to submit the totality of our humanity to God so that He may shape our character and understanding of His nature.

Prophets actively allow God to humble them so that they may be filled to a greater extent with the character and nature of Christ. This was certainly the prophet Habakkuk's heart when he wrote, *"I will stand my watch and set myself apart on the rampart, and watch to see what He will say to me, and what I will answer when I am corrected"* (Habakkuk 2:1, NIV). Habakkuk lowered his pride and positioned his heart to receive the Lord's correction. This allowed him to directly receive the Word of God and minister powerfully to God's people.

Prophets recognize that the sustenance of life itself is the very Word of God, which energizes our mind, body, and spirit. This "Word of God" is not the ink on the pages of the Bible, but the living and active voice of the Holy Spirit. This is what sustains us and empowers us to live within the will and intent of the Father. Jesus, the greatest prophet, testified to this reality of divine sustenance and empowerment:

> "'My food,' said Jesus, 'is to do the will of him who sent me and to finish his work.'" John 4:34 (NIV)

A saying I love to live by is "a teacher is always teaching." This is in regard to the Holy Spirit instructing us in the ways of the Father and of Jesus Christ. He is our ever-present rabbi, our omnipresent teacher. God teaches us through the Bible, of course, but He also speaks constantly through daily life experiences. Prophets are those who believe this reality and strive to live in a flow of understanding what God is saying and doing. It's a bit of a cliché at this point, but I really do believe there are no coincidences. Prophets are excellent at recognizing God's hand behind seemingly mundane, everyday events. They then draw conclusions and speak forth what they feel God is doing, based on their past experiences and their familiarity with God's way of operating.

One example (of many) from my own life is that, for many months now, I have found the number 316 pervasively appearing. Rarely a day will pass when I do not see this number pop up in some way in life. I find myself looking at the clock exactly at 3:16 nearly every day, even though I do not strive to do so. I see the number on cars, on trucks, on mailboxes, on cash registers. When I see this number, John 3:16 immediately pops into my head. It is a subtle reminder to me that God loves the world and plans on redeeming it. When I see these numbers, He reminds me that I have a mission and a part to play in His grand story. I am reminded to love deeply because I myself am seen and known. These miniature "teaching moments" allow me to reset myself back into His presence.

The anointing, God's very presence, is the sustenance of His prophetic people. It allows us to live in a flow of revelation that empowers new creation kingdom living. It constantly teaches us, conforming us more and more to the image of Jesus Christ. When we abide and saturate in this presence, we gain access to the living Word of God, who brings abundant life into every area of our being. To be away from this presence is to live in a state of death, a pattern of spiritual regression. I resonate with Peter's words to Jesus: *"Lord, to whom shall we go? You have the words of eternal life"* (John 6:68, NIV). There is no other way to live.

***

In this chapter, we learned that we are called to carry the presence of Jesus Christ with us wherever we go. This presence is enabled by the anointing of the Holy Spirit and activated by the mind of Christ. We have the treasure of God's empowering presence operating in and through our weak humanity. Although once dead (literally: not existing) in our sin, God made us alive through the Holy Spirit. He has seated us in heavenly places alongside His Son, Jesus. The image of God within humanity - once stained, tarnished, and imprisoned by the power of sin - has been recovered by Jesus Christ, who lives within. We are now being progressively renewed in the experiential knowledge and image of the Creator.[13] The anointing teaches us to walk in the ways of Christ, who is the prototype of the new humanity. The old has gone, the new is here!

We carry around in our bodies the eternal life of Jesus Christ. This eternal life flows out from the center of our being into our physical and spiritual environments. To those who long to learn the truth and love God, this eternal life gives off a pleasing spiritual aroma. To those who reject God's love, it is an aroma of death and judgment.[14] This anointing permeates and saturates every area of our being. We no longer live for and to ourselves. Christ now lives in us, working through us to accomplish His mission of universal redemption and reconciliation.

The mind of Christ is the tool by which God's prophetic people access and manifest the life of heaven. It is the means by which God shares His mind and heart with us, teaching us how to walk in the way of Truth. The scriptures instruct us to abide in the anointing in order to walk in the same manner as Jesus. Jesus modeled a lifestyle of total obedience to the Holy Spirit and the will of the Father. His purpose was to release over people what the Father was saying and doing in the heavenly realm.

The anointing teaches us all things that pertain to holiness, purity, and power. As we learn to actively abide in it, to recognize God's all-permeating presence, we are experientially discipled by the Holy Spirit in the ways of God. God's prophets live in a constant, continual state of spiritual

---

[13] "Put on the new self, which is being renewed in knowledge in the image of its Creator." Colossians 3:10 (NIV)

[14] "But thanks be to God, who always leads us as captives in Christ's triumphal procession and uses us to spread the aroma of the knowledge of him everywhere. For we are to God the pleasing aroma of Christ among those who are being saved and those who are perishing. To the one we are an aroma that brings death; to the other, an aroma that brings life." 2 Corinthians 2:14-16 (NIV)

teachability. They have surrendered their perception and understanding of reality into the hands of the One who is reality itself.

Now, the mandate of God's kingdom prophets is threefold: carry, identify with, and release the presence of Jesus Christ. We have learned that we are carriers of the eternal life, but what does it mean to fully identify with and resonate with this life? Our ability to fully identify with the mind of Christ and the heart of God the Father is what precedes our ability to fully release God's presence.

Chapter Three

Identifiers

At the heart of the gospel message is God's desire to seek and save His lost and misguided children. John 3:16 says, *"For God so loved the world that He gave His only unique son, that whoever believes in Him shall not die but have eternal life."* This is probably the most popular verse in the Bible, but we must not separate it from what immediately follows: *"For God did not send his Son into the world to condemn the world, but to save the world through him."*

God did not send His Son to condemn the world. The Son came to rescue the world, and not just humanity, but the entire cosmos. Salvation is therefore restoration and renewal - an imbuement with the eternal life of God. We have made Christianity a philosophical system of right and wrong. We have reduced a radical, life-altering spirituality into a program of intellectual assent. This breeds feelings of exclusivity and fear. Because of this belief paradigm, outsiders, those not yet in Christ, are treated with subtle contempt and derision. Our religious pride often blinds us to this reality. The hidden, self-righteous attitude empowering Christian mission has become: "I have something you need. Therefore, you are less than me. I will make you my 'project' until you learn to believe exactly what I believe. Then, you will finally know what God's love looks and feels like."

Our "evangelism" has become a global effort to "convert" the nations of the world to a religious ideology and a set of prescribed ideas and behaviors. We are in error to think that this is what the Bible means when it asks us to call the Gentiles to the obedience of the faith and make disciples of all nations.

Evangelism that is not empowered and directed by God's love is not evangelism, but religious activity that fuels our self-righteous attitudes and veiled spiritual insecurities. Our call to make non-believers obedient to the faith is dependent on our ability to identify with and transmit the heart of God to them. If we do not have love, we are nothing. God is love. His power flows through love and love only. Powerful people in the kingdom are those who love deeply and authentically.

God's prophetic people not only carry the presence of God and the mind of Christ, but resonate and identify with the heart of the Father. This is what allows us to represent Christ and effectively release His kingdom. The heart of the Father is deep unconditional love for His creation. He is passionate about saving us from sin and death and will go to any length to do so. The Father desires all to be saved and to come to a knowledge of the truth.[15] He is not interested in spiritual arrogance and religiosity.

Many Christians can articulate these realities, but the purity and health of a tree is always made known by the quality of its fruit. We can talk about the love of God all day long, but do we manifest it in genuine love and action on behalf of God and our neighbor? If we take an honest look at the Body of Christ today, it is evident we prioritize knowledge about God over and above an experience of His presence. Why? Because knowledge and words are easy. In an unbelieving world, knowledge is power. This is why education and factual learning are so highly valued. The more I know, the more valuable I become in the eyes of others who seek the same type of knowledge. This is why we have such respect for "experts" in different fields. We value them because their knowledge can in turn give us knowledge, which we feel can make us more valuable in the eyes of others. This is how the world thinks and operates.

---

[15] "God our Savior wants all people to be saved and to come to a knowledge of the truth." 1 Timothy 2:4-5 (NIV)

"The Lord is not slow in keeping his promise, as some understand slowness. Instead he is patient with you, not wanting anyone to perish, but everyone to come to repentance." 2 Peter 3:9 (NIV)

Love, on the other hand, is difficult. It requires sacrifice, risk, and deep vulnerability. It is a narrow way, and few find it. Even fewer walk on it. None of us have perfected it. Love requires us to face our fears and insecurities and to present them before others. Learning love is painful because it requires spiritual process and a slow death of the ego (the "flesh" in New Testament writings). Love is suffering. There is no guarantee we will ever receive anything in return. Unlike knowledge, love does not create any sort of value that we can retain and later leverage for our own benefit. It is entirely selfless. Learning love requires focused spiritual effort.

The Church today abounds in knowledge. We take comfort in our ideologies, theologies, and established understandings of the character and nature of God. We have sacrificed love at the altar of knowledge, because knowledge is power. Knowledge about God creates in us a false feeling of spiritual security and power. We think, "I know about God. I think the right things about Him. Therefore, I am saved and will go to heaven one day." Love then becomes obedient to our knowledge. It becomes a performance. We start loving because we feel like we are supposed to. When this happens, we only love others because our intellectual faith demands it. We do not love genuinely, organically, and whole-heartedly. Our theological knowledge sets a boundary for our ability to love.[16]

It is impossible for prophets to truly love others without first fully identifying with the life, death, and resurrection of Christ. Comprehending the totality of Christ's sacrifice on the cross is what enables and empowers our ability to resonate with and love others. Without a deep and genuine personal revelation of the Father's love for us, all of our activity on God's behalf is merely religious striving for His approval. When we have a revelation of our full identification with Jesus Christ, we become confident in our ability and potential to act as His representatives on earth.

As He Is, So Are We

Prophets carry a revelation of their synergistic union with the ascended Christ. This metaphysical reality frightens and offends religionists, but it is an

---

[16] "Jesus said, 'If you were blind, you would not be guilty of sin; but now that you claim you can see, your guilt remains.'" John 9:41 (NIV)

essential component of the anointing. Synergy is the interaction and cooperation of two agents to create a combined effect greater than the sum of their separate effects. As we learned from Ephesians 2, we were "dead" in our sins and transgressions, but we have been made "alive" and sit with Christ in heavenly places. "Heavenly places" may provoke wonderful mental imagery of an extraordinary existence beyond this life. Again, this is to read the text divorced from a first-century Jewish worldview. To be "seated with Christ in heavenly places" means that, in Christ, God has united the human spirit with the Holy Spirit in order to bring our realm of existence into alignment with God's ("Here as in heaven" from the Lord's Prayer). Having been sealed with the Holy Spirit, believers work with God to continue and ultimately finish the work of the ascended Christ, who objectively destroyed the power of sin and death on the cross. We have been drawn into His fullness in order to accomplish His mission.

Our heavenly union with Christ is predicated on another spiritual reality: our old self, the part of us that belonged to the old creation order that is passing away, died with Jesus Christ on the cross. Having been made alive in Him, we now serve as a new humanity through which His power flows into the earthly realm. The part of our humanity that belonged to the old creation order was effectively destroyed by Christ on the cross. We died to our old sinful nature and, thus, to the spiritual forces of wickedness that dominated in the realm of the old creation.

> "Don't you know that all of us who were baptized into Christ Jesus were baptized into his death? We were therefore buried with him through baptism into death in order that, just as Christ was raised from the dead through the glory of the Father, we too may live a new life." Romans 6:3-4 (NIV)

> "Your whole self ruled by the flesh (the old creation reality) was put off when you were circumcised by Christ, having been buried with him in baptism (into death), in which you were also raised with him through your faith in the working of God, who raised him from the dead. When you were dead in your sins and in the uncircumcision of your flesh, God made you alive with Christ… And having disarmed

the powers and authorities, he made a public spectacle of them, triumphing over them by the cross" Colossians 2:11-13,15 (NIV), parenthetical annotations mine

We were baptized (immersed) into death with Christ but have effectively been made alive with Him because He was raised from the dead. Christ did not just die for us, but *as* us. Jesus, as the son of God, represented all of humanity in His life, death, and resurrection. It is hard to grasp or imagine, but you and I were with Him on the cross. In fact, all of humanity was, because Jesus bore the sins of all humanity within His body.[17] This is the kind of understanding that informed the apostles' reality when they were writing their letters, so it should inform ours as well.

God Himself confirmed this truth by pouring out the Holy Spirit, His eternal life, upon all humanity on the day of Pentecost. Our faith, therefore, becomes a matter of trusting and believing in what Jesus has already accomplished on the cross. When we do, we "receive" the Holy Spirit and enter into our new creation identity as God's sons and daughters. We become miniature working models of the new creation who fully identify with the risen Christ.

The objection that may naturally arise is: "Are you trying to say that God needs humans to accomplish His purposes? God is all-sovereign. He doesn't need us." This is true. God does not need us. However, in love, He has included us in His grand plan for the universe. We are the "firstfruits" of the new creation - the spiritual prophets, priests, and kings of the coming ages. We are God's "masterpieces." He has prepared good works for us to walk in that bring about the kingdom "on earth as it is in heaven."[18] This synergistic union, the flowing together of the divine with the merely human, is how this will be accomplished. Our union with God points to Christ, who was fully God and fully man. Although not inherently divine, humanity now partakes

---

[17] "He himself bore our sins in his body on the cross, so that we might die to sins and live for righteousness; by his wounds you have been healed." 1 Peter 2:24 (NIV)

"For Christ's love compels us, because we are convinced that one died for all, and therefore all died." 2 Corinthians 5:14 (NIV)

[18] "For we are God's handiwork, created in Christ Jesus to do good works, which God prepared in advance for us to do." Ephesians 2:10 (NIV)

of the divine nature.[19] In this sense we are Christ-ones, "Christians." The joining of our human nature with the Holy Spirit of God is a reality that glorifies Christ.

"See what great love the Father has lavished on us, that we should be called children of God! And that is what we are!" These incredible words were written by the apostle John in his first Epistle. 1 John is an incredible book of the Bible that was written many years after Christ's ascension into heaven. John had been meditating on the fullness of Christ's work for decades. John is clearly writing from a place of deep awareness of his status as a beloved son of God and a member of the new creation.

And what is John's main focus in this letter after so many years of revelation and experiences with the Holy Spirit? *Love.* It is such a concern for him that the word appears 46 times in five relatively short chapters. Love is the atmosphere of God's kingdom. It enables and empowers everything that God does, for God is love. *"Dear friends, let us love one another, for love comes from God. Everyone who loves has been born of God and knows God. Whoever does not love does not know God, because God is love,"* John writes in 1 John 4:7. The authority and power of the kingdom flow through love alone.

The profound mystery of our death and resurrection with Jesus Christ should first and foremost lead us to love our neighbor more deeply. God trusts us with much and those who have been given a trust must prove faithful. We are alive with Christ and seated with Him in the heavenly realms, but the throne we sit on is one of love. God's current rule and reign is not one of worldly might and power, but of love. We have been adopted into God's family and given the status of sons and daughters to experience His love and diffuse this love to all around us.

"As Jesus is, so are we in this world," John writes in 1 John 4:17 (NKJV). And what does it mean to be like Jesus? It is to live free from fear and sin, in a full revelation of our identity as God's sons and daughters, ready to serve

---

[19] "Through these he has given us his very great and precious promises, so that through them you may participate in the divine nature, having escaped the corruption in the world caused by evil desires." 2 Peter 1:4 (NIV)

humanity in any and every possible way. As we walk on this path of love, we destroy the works of the enemy and pave the way for the kingdom of God.[20]

Like a wife who has been united to her husband in mind, body, and will, the Church is now in union with the ascended Christ. The anointing of the Holy Spirit is the wedding band that testifies to this union. In this new creation marriage, we have been given a new name, that of Jesus Christ. We have died to ourselves and now live in full living submission to our Husband. Everything we do as New Testament prophets, priests, and kings flows from this incredible reality.

The Prophetic Burden

Christ is our model and pattern. Jesus desired to fully identify with a lost and broken humanity. His heart was and is for us. This burden of love brought Him to action. He took on human form and walked amongst us. His desire is that we would open our eyes to the reality of His love and walk in our divine inheritance.

> "In your relationships with one another, have the same mindset as Christ Jesus: Who, being in very nature God, did not consider equality with God something to be used to his own advantage; rather, he made himself nothing by taking the very nature of a servant, being made in human likeness. And being found in appearance as a man, he humbled himself by becoming obedient to death - even death on a cross!" Philippians 2:6-8 (NIV)

God's prophetic people live aware of their union with Christ and the blessings of this union, but it is always a means to an end. This end is identification with and love for humanity. We are called to *do*, to act on behalf of our fellow humans in order to tangibly manifest the kingdom of God. God burdened Himself, He condescended on our behalf so that we could live in union with Him. There was an identification with us, a burden, and an action.

---

[20] "And it will be said: 'Build up, build up, prepare the road! Remove the obstacles out of the way of my people.'" Isaiah 57:14 (NIV)

The Holy Spirit makes us aware of problems that lay heavy on God's heart. By carrying one another's burdens, we fulfill the law of Christ.[21] Like Christ, prophetic people are chosen to carry specific burdens on behalf of the people. Deep empathy, compassion, and concern for our fellow humans is not something that comes naturally to most. How does God work to grow these Christ-like qualities within us?

God invites prophets into experiences that grow in us a deeper understanding of His heart for humanity. It may be a severe spiritual trial where we come face to face with our own brokenness, a profound experience of inner healing, or a divine encounter that flips our understanding of the world upside down. God may ask us to do things that fall far beyond the lines of our established comfort zones. He may ask us to sacrifice relationships, careers, or coveted possessions. Why? He works through these experiences to bring us to see reality from His perspective.

I call these difficult experiences the "Valley of Trouble." God's design is that we would not stay in them for long, but He uses them to build our identity in Christ and shape the future of our divine calling. We sacrifice our own strength and learn to lean exclusively on Him. We emerge from these valleys empowered by the Holy Spirit to accomplish what He has called us to. This is the biblical promise that accompanies the prophetic calling.

> "I am going to allure her; I will lead her into the wilderness and speak tenderly to her. There I will give her back her vineyards and will make the Valley of Trouble a door of hope. There she will sing as in the days of her youth." Hosea 2:15 (NIV)

The Old Testament prophets offer fascinating case studies of the prophetic burden. These men chose to sacrifice the totality of their being to the living God. As a result, they were consumed by the Word of God. They became perfectly submissive instruments, prepared to do any work on the Lord's behalf.

---

[21] "Carry each other's burdens, and in this way you will fulfill the law of Christ." Galatians 6:2 (NIV)

A standout example for our present topic is the prophet Hosea. God asked Hosea to marry a prostitute, who would later prove to be unfaithful. Despite this, Hosea continued to love her. Although it pained him greatly, this experience allowed Hosea to deeply resonate with God's heart for a disobedient Israel. Hosea's ability to fully identify with God's heart grew in him greater concern and empathy for a nation in turmoil. As a result, his words carried great power and authority, so much so that we still have them today!

I myself have been led by God through the "Valley of Trouble." It was a three-year journey of intense spiritual battle, inner healing, and radical experiences with the presence of God. This experience was painful but as God led me through the healing process, I realized I was gaining valuable tools and insights to set other spiritual captives free from their various bondages. The pain and confusion built within me a heart of compassion, empathy, and resonance for those lost in death and darkness. God gave me a revelation of His heart. I now live with a burden to see people set free and living in the fullness and freedom of the resurrection life. This was a difficult experience that radically changed my life. I gave up my career, major relationships, and my life dreams. I have become consumed with the Word of God. There has never been a desire in me to go back to what once was. I feel compelled to press on, straining for what lies ahead in God's grand plan.

Without the constant empowering presence of the Holy Spirit, the prophetic burden can become overwhelming. We can become prone to hopelessness, despair, and depression. King Solomon wrote, *"For with much wisdom comes much sorrow; the more knowledge, the more grief"* (Ecclesiastes 1:18, NIV. It is a powerful thing to see the world's problems from God's perspective, but it is not always pleasant. However, He shows us because He has prepared us to handle it and He trusts us to partner with Him in the solution. His yoke is easy, and His burden is light.

Signs and Symbols

During His time on earth, one of Jesus' favorite designations for Himself was "son of man." This term carries more weight than we may initially realize. Old Testament prophets such as Daniel and Ezekiel are also specified as "sons of man" in the scriptures. These "sons of man" were specifically chosen by God to appear and speak before the people.

The expression "son of man" occurs a whopping 81 times in the four gospels. The Greek word for son is *huios*. Its meaning extends far beyond the biological. In Greek thinking (remember we are aiming to think from a first-century perspective), to be a "son" is to embody a concept or idea. In the Bible, we can read about "sons of thunder," "sons of disobedience," "sons of God," etc. A "son" represents something.

Jesus is the son of God in the sense that He is the most perfect representation of the heavenly Father,[22] but He is also the son of man in that He is a *living representative of all humanity*. Jesus assumed the sins of humanity on the cross, died, and was raised to new life. In doing so, He overhauled human nature by destroying the power of sin and death. He is the archetype, the prototype, the "firstfruit" of a new humanity. This new humanity experiences restored union with God and is characterized by the presence of His Holy Spirit.

God's children, those who have received the promise of the Holy Spirit through faith, have become "sons of God." Obviously, we are not God's biological children, but His spiritual children. Empowered by the Holy Spirit, we now live to represent His character and nature. The word "son" implies a full identification with something. Unlike Christ, we are not fully divine beings. We are human beings who have been given the ability to partake of the divine nature. We are ultimately *human*, but our humanity has become energized by His divinity. We are not the same essence as God, but His radiating energies imbue our mortal existence.[23] God's presence is the hallmark of the new creation and the new humanity.

We are the sons of God, but, like the Old Testament prophets before us, we are also the sons of humanity. Our lives themselves are a sign and symbol of what God is doing and intends to do through mankind. Speaking of God's children, the prophet Isaiah says, *"Here am I, and the children the Lord has given me. We are signs and symbols in Israel from the Lord Almighty, who dwells on Mount*

---

[22] "The Son is the image of the invisible God, the firstborn over all creation." Colossians 1:15 (NIV)
[23] See Peter 1:4 in footnote 19.

Zion" (Isaiah 8:18, NIV). This means we represent humanity and what greater humanity as a whole will one day become: human beings who experience restored relationship with God and access to His divine presence. We are miniature working models of the new creation. We remain incomplete in our human nature, but will be clothed one day with immorality - the fully divinized human body. We may in fact "die" and leave the body, but God has promised us a physical resurrection in which we will, like Christ, experience the glory of a fully divinized body.[24]

The Body of Christ is a sign of the age to come. In fact, we already partake of the "powers of the age to come" through the Holy Spirit.[25] We are simultaneously participants in the age of the old creation order that is currently passing away and the age that is to come, the "age of ages" in which God's kingdom will be fully consummated on the earth and His plans and purposes for the universe will be brought to completion and fulfillment. At that time, God will become all in all.

Christ's death and resurrection have already passed judgment on the age of the old creation. That age - full of sin, delusion, disorder, and death - has already begun to pass away. The restoration of all things, the "new creation" has already begun. The promise of the new creation can already be seen in Christ's new humanity that has been saved out of the "present evil age" that is passing away. Again, this understanding informed the apostles' reality and it should inform and enlighten ours as well.

> "Grace and peace to you from God our Father and the Lord Jesus Christ, **who gave himself for our sins to rescue us from the present evil age**, according to the will of our God and Father." Galatians 1:4 (NIV)

---

[24] "So will it be with the resurrection of the dead. The body that is sown is perishable, it is raised imperishable; it is sown in dishonor, it is raised in glory; it is sown in weakness, it is raised in power; it is sown a natural body, it is raised a spiritual body. If there is a natural body, there is also a spiritual body." 1 Corinthians 15:42-44 (NIV)

[25] See Hebrews 6:5.

> "What I mean, brothers and sisters, is that the time is short. From now on those who have wives should live as if they did not; those who mourn, as if they did not; those who are happy, as if they were not; those who buy something, as if it were not theirs to keep; those who use the things, as if not engrossed in them. **For this world in its present form is passing away.**" 1 Corinthians 7:29-31 (NIV)

God's prophetic people live between the ages. We identify with the age that is passing away for the sake of those still lost in sin and darkness. We identify with the age to come in order to energize and empower Christian mission. Our faith must be Spirit-empowered and Spirit-dominated. In Christ, God has made available to us the riches of heaven and the abundant life of the Father. As God's prophets, we freely access these blessings through relationship with Jesus. Certainly, the kingdom of God is "already, but not yet." But what will empower and spurn the Church to action is the seeking and seizing of the "already." The kingdom of heaven is at hand, and we are called to forcefully lay hold of it.

***

In this chapter, we explored what it means for God's prophetic people to identify with Jesus Christ and His presence. Our old self ruled by the flesh was put to death on the cross.[26] As God's new creation, we have been spiritually raised to life with Christ. In the Holy Spirit, we "sit" with Christ in the heavenly realms in order to partner with Him in the advancement of His kingdom. This union with Christ allows spiritual blessings to flow from His realm of existence (heaven) into ours (earth).

Our full identification with the death and resurrection of Christ means we also submit our lives to our fellow humans. God is love. Without love, there is no kingdom of heaven. The greatest expressions of Christ, the most obvious

---

[26] "Your whole self ruled by the flesh was put off when you were circumcised by Christ." Colossians 2:11 (NIV)

"For we know that our old self was crucified with him so that the body ruled by sin might be done away with, that we should no longer be slaves to sin – because anyone who has died has been set free from sin." Romans 6:6 (NIV)

displays of His kingdom, are loving deeds. As the apostle John wrote, *"greater love has no one than this: to lay down one's life for one's friends"* (John 15:13, NIV).

Love is the goal of the spiritual path. God increases our capacity to love and empathize with others by leading us through trials and experiences that increase our empathy, compassion, and ability to see people through the eyes of Christ. We cannot love until we have a personal revelation of His love for us. We love because He first loved us. Christ will not be made known to the world through displays of power or intellectual arguments, but by our ability and capacity to love deeply and richly. In the words of the Master, Jesus Christ, *"By this everyone will know that you are my disciples, if you love one another"* (John 13:35, NIV).

The prophetic anointing empowers God's people to carry, identify with, and release His presence into the world. We are living signs and symbols of the reality of the new creation. Having firmly established what it means for new creation prophets to carry and identify with the presence of Jesus Christ, we are ready to explore the more tangible dimension of the prophetic anointing: the releasing of God's presence.

Chapter Four

Releasers

Today's world is obsessed with the fantastic. The last few decades have featured a massive explosion of interest in fantasy, science fiction, and larger-than-life characters. We love elaborate stories that pit unassuming heroes against seemingly unstoppable evil forces that threaten to overwhelm and crush all that is good. We resonate with these heroes because they share our humanity. We find ourselves cheering for them as they overcome their weaknesses, fears, and insecurities to gain victory.

At the root of these stories, there is often some sort of power source that the protagonists discover and tap into in order to tip the scales in their favor. Perhaps it is God or a god-like being, some sort of magic, or a latent inherent power that is developed slowly over time as the story progresses. This plot element is what often makes or breaks a great story!

Our modern religious and spiritual practices have certainly been influenced by this thirst for the phenomenal, mystical, and esoteric. New Age spirituality (a modern approach to paganism, astrology, divination, spirit channeling, and energy healing, among other things) has taken our world by storm. Eastern spiritual practices, such as yoga and meditation, now dominate the Western landscape. Meanwhile, forms of Christianity that emphasize a direct experience of God and the gifts of the Holy Spirit are exploding around the world. For a modern-day Christian deeply entrenched in intellectual faith and an established understanding of the Bible, these developments may seem terrifying. What is happening? Where is God? Are these the "end times?"

What we can see happening both in the world and the Church today is only a symptom of a deeper issue: *religion does not work*. What I mean by "religion" is intellectual precepts, doctrines, and patterns of teaching that are supposed to keep us connected to the living God. Religion has done a phenomenal job at teaching us how to obey. We know how to obey God. What we are more clueless about is how to genuinely love and experience Him.

Intellectual religion is like concrete that gets poured over a field of wildflowers. It may take time, but sooner or later the flowers will find a way to break through the surface. This is what Christ's Spirit is doing today. He is breaking His Body out of rigid intellectual faith paradigms and leading us into a direct experience of His love, presence, and power. This does not at all mean that doctrine or intellectual truths of the faith are bad or unnecessary. We need doctrine and we need proper knowledge. However, they are pillars that support a direct experience of God. An experience of God's love must empower our knowledge. The Body of Christ today has so much intellectual knowledge. Intellectual knowledge and arguments about the faith don't transform anyone. A direct experience of God's presence and love do.

We have learned *what* to believe and *how* to believe, but we have lost *why* we believe. Religion and its (usually) well-intentioned thought leaders have taught us that the crux of Christianity, the reason for the Christian faith, is to be obedient in order to please God. Church has become about leaders feeding us information so that we can ultimately increase our obedience. After all, doesn't the Bible say that if we love God, we will obey His commandments?

The issue is we are still caught in a performance mentality: *if* I obey, I can increase my awareness of God and His presence. *If* I learn about the Bible and its truths, I can be pleasing to God and walk in His ways. There is obviously truth to this, but we often place the cart before the horse. This intellectual faith paradigm is exhausting, inauthentic, and death-bringing. This neo-legalism is why so many young people have left and are leaving the Church today. It is also why New Age and neo-pagan spirituality has exploded. They are attempts to meet humanity's genuine thirst for an experience of God.

We love because He first loved us, not the other way around. I act and behave as a son of God because I *want* to, not because I *have* to. Our behavior changes naturally as we learn about who we have become in Christ Jesus. He already trusts all Christians to carry His presence and release the realities of His realm. When this revelation comes, when we hear this word of Truth, we are changed forever. This is what this book is about - to awaken believers to a new way of thinking. It is not so much about *what* to think, but *how* to think. We have the mind of Christ. What to think about Christ is obviously important, but how to think like Him even more so.

To those whom God has given much, much more will be demanded. As God's children, we have already been blessed with the reality of His eternal life. This eternal life flows out from the core of our being into our everyday lives. We are His new temple, the place of His manifest presence. We have not been given access to the very presence of God simply for our own well-being. The presence of God is for everyone. It is a blessing to be shared freely.

I immediately think of the miraculous feeding of the 4,000 and 5,000 in the gospel accounts. Jesus blesses the few loaves of bread and gives them to the disciples to distribute. The bread symbolizes the presence of God. Jesus entrusts the disciples to disperse the bread in order to feed the crowds. The Lord does not do it Himself. It was the disciples' responsibility to distribute what they have been given from the Lord.

A heavenly mandate of the prophetic anointing is to release the presence of Jesus Christ. Our call to release this presence is where intellectual faith meets experiential risk, where theory collides with praxis. It is where we step into our roles as heavenly ambassadors and change agents for the kingdom of God. The world is desperate for a tangible experience of Jesus Christ and His love. This experience must extend beyond mere words and religious platitudes.

"The kingdom of God is not a matter of talk, but of power," Paul writes in 1 Corinthians 4:20. This verse is appropriate for our present topic, but it requires some qualification. These words tend to be removed from their context and used as a biblical proof-text for miracle-filled Christian living. Miracles are important, yes, and they will be discussed in this chapter.

However, Paul is not trying to claim some sort of superior spiritual power and ability that sets him above the rest of Christ's followers. He is making the point that *the kingdom is not an intellectual kingdom*. Its power does not derive from ideas about God, impressive philosophies, and flashy rhetoric. Rather, it manifests from the new humanity's ability to *do* and *act* as the Body of Jesus Christ. This is God's power - to manifest His love through an inexhaustible array of deeds and actions that reveal the character and nature of Jesus Christ.

I like to think of the Christian faith as a tool belt with many different loops, hooks, and compartments. The belt itself represents the love of Christ. His love is what holds and supports the other tools, allowing us to use them. These tools are the spiritual gifts and graces of the Holy Spirit. I think most Christians today have a toolbelt with one giant compartment called "Bible knowledge." When problems arise inside and outside of the Church that can't be solved by simply quoting a Bible verse, we are powerless. Something else may be required.

This "something else" is the perfect will of the Father - what He is saying and doing over any given situation in any particular moment. Jesus Christ, our model and pattern, carried with Him a full spiritual tool belt. He did what the Father was doing and said what the Father was saying. The pages of the gospels are filled with Jesus initiating unusual miracles, casting out demons, discerning heart postures, dispensing wisdom, and spending time with the loathsome and unwanted dregs of society. Jesus' love was not limited to kind words and actions. He had the full resources of heaven at His disposal and He was not afraid to use them.

Jesus lived within the perfect will of the Father. This allowed Him to flow in an "on earth as it is in heaven" lifestyle that He prayed we would emulate:

> "'Our Father in heaven, hallowed be your name, your kingdom come, your will be done, on earth as it is in heaven.'" Matthew 6:9-10 (**NIV**)

On earth as it is in heaven. This is to make the present realities of God's realm manifest in ours. And what is God's reality? Simply put, it is love, joy, peace, patience, kindness, goodness, gentleness, faithfulness, and self-control. Psalm

119:89 says that the Lord's word is "settled in heaven." Through the Holy Spirit, God's prophetic people access this Word in order to manifest the realities of God's realm here on earth. The ultimate goal is that God and His love may be all in all.

The kingdom of heaven must be realized within each of us before we can manifest it externally. This is why Jesus said, *"The coming of the kingdom of God is not something that can be observed, nor will people say, 'Here it is,' or 'There it is,' because the kingdom of God is within you"* (Luke 17:20-21, NIV) and Paul could write," *The kingdom of God is not a matter of eating and drinking* (tangible things), *but of righteousness, peace and joy in the Holy Spirit"* (Romans 14:17, NIV).

In God's anointed people, the Word of God is "made flesh" – it is internally realized. Our destiny is to become miniature working models of Jesus Christ. This is possible because the Holy Spirit lives within us and we carry God's eternal life, as we established earlier. The scriptures call Jesus the "first of many brethren."[27] Having been adopted into God's family, we now live as righteous ("right-standing") sons and daughters who lack nothing necessary to accomplish the will of the Father. We have access to every spiritual blessing, grace and gift in the heavenly realms that enable us to realize and manifest the kingdom.

This chapter explores the third responsibility of God's prophetic people: release the presence of Jesus Christ. I do not doubt this section of this book may at first seem unattainable or controversial for Christians new to the more "experiential" dimensions of the Christian faith. I want to assure readers that nothing I write is mere theory or speculation - I actively live in the realities I attempt to describe, and I know many others who do so as well. My life is saturated with miracles and gifts of the Spirit. My intention is not to portray myself as spiritually superior in any way. My heart has always been to seek and live in the "more" of God and I am passionate about sharing this reality with others. My prayer is that we awaken to what Jesus Christ has already given us. If we stand against fear and are willing to step outside the box of our fixed religious understanding, we will be surprised. The reality of His presence is beyond anything we could ever ask for or imagine.

---

[27] "For those whom He foreknew, He also predestined to become conformed to the image of His Son, so that He would be the firstborn among many brethren." Romans 8:29 (NASB)

Open Heavens

We will begin by exploring the concept of an "open heaven." Because of our union with Christ through the Holy Spirit, all believers have access to this spiritual reality. An open heaven is where the realities and resources of God's realm flow freely into our lives so that we may be equipped for works of love.

> "Praise be to the God and Father of our Lord Jesus Christ, **who has blessed us in the heavenly realms with every spiritual blessing in Christ**. For he chose us in him before the creation of the world to be holy and blameless in his sight. In love he predestined us for adoption to sonship through Jesus Christ...With all wisdom and understanding, he made known to us the mystery of his will according to his good pleasure, which he purposed in Christ, to be put into effect when the times reach their fulfillment - **to bring unity to all things in heaven and on earth under Christ**." Ephesians 1:3-10 (NIV)

Notice the clear heaven-meets-earth and sonship language in this passage from Ephesians: *heavenly realms, spiritual blessings, adoption, unity to all things in heaven and on earth under Christ.* The point of our position in Christ is to bring union and unity between the heavenly and the earthly. How is this accomplished? Spiritual blessings from an open heaven.

Where does the concept of an "open heaven" come from? We have established that the Body of Christ has become the new temple of the living God, the location of God's manifest presence. This new temple is the open door between God's realm ("heaven") and our reality ("earth"). The forgiveness of sin on the cross is what has enabled humanity's extraordinary access to the heavenly storehouses. I would like to mention two notable examples of open heavens from the scriptures that inform our present understanding of the prophetic anointing.

The first is Jacob's visionary experience in Genesis 28. Jacob, grandson of Abraham, flees from his brother Esau into the wilderness. There, he lays down to rest and soon finds himself in a visionary experience in which he beholds a stairway linking heaven and earth. On this stairway, Jacob sees angels ascending and descending between the two realms. He then sees the Lord, who tells him, "*I am the Lord, the God of your father Abraham and the God of Isaac. I will give you and your descendants the land on which you are lying...all peoples on earth will be blessed through you and your offspring...I am with you and will watch over you wherever you go, and I will bring you back to this land.*" Jacob awakes in amazement and thinks, "*Surely the Lord is in this place, and I was not aware of it. How awesome is this place! This is none other than the house of God; this is the gate of heaven.*" Jacob then sets up a pillar in this strange and special place. He anoints the pillar with oil and names the location "Bethel" which means "house of God."

There are some key considerations in this story. First, Jacob is from the lineage of Abraham. This means he is a *child of promise* - God will eventually produce a family of descendants through him who will be richly blessed both spiritually and physically (these promises are outlined throughout the book of Genesis). Secondly, there is clear heaven-meets-earth imagery and language in this story. Jacob experiences an open heaven where the reality of heaven meets the reality of earth. Angels, God's messengers, facilitate this interaction. Thirdly, Jacob anoints a pillar at the location as a gesture to denote "sacred" space. He calls this sacred space the "house of God."

Hopefully, the connections between Jacob and us are already becoming clear. Being in Christ, we are from the spiritual lineage of Jacob, who was a distant ancestor of Jesus. We have access to the same promises God made to Abraham and his grandson Jacob because of Christ, who has blessed us with every spiritual blessing in the heavenly realms. As the new temple, we are the current "house of God." God has anointed us with the Holy Spirit. The entire human being is now a "sacred space." The Holy Spirit is our connection to God's realm. Angels, God's ministering spirits sent to those who will inherit salvation, now freely descend upon us and ascend back into God's realm.[28] We lack nothing for accomplishing God's purposes on earth. All things are ours. Remember, we are seated in the "heavenly places" with Christ Jesus. This reality is why Paul could write lofty and exalted words full of promise about God's newly formed Spirit-people:

---

[28] "Are not all angels ministering spirits sent to serve those who will inherit salvation." Hebrews 1:14 (NIV)

> "So then, no more boasting about human leaders! All things are yours, whether Paul or Apollos or Cephas or the world or life or death or the present or the future - all are yours, and you are of Christ, and Christ is of God." 1 Corinthians 3:21-23 (NIV)

Another example of an open heaven from Scripture that is relevant to our topic is the baptism of Jesus Christ. We might understand Jacob's story from the Old Testament as a standalone supernatural experience if not for the fact that Jesus' baptism is a clear and obvious allusion to it. Christ's baptism strengthens the idea that we can experience an open heaven just like Jacob did.

Jesus' public ministry is preceded by his baptism at the hands of John the Baptist. John the Baptist was the last prophet to Israel before the arrival of the kingdom of God in and through the person of Jesus Christ. There is deep significance in this: the last prophet of the old-world order baptizes the first prophet of the new kingdom age, who is our model and pattern. This is the turning point in humanity's spiritual history. The new creation, the restoration of all things is at hand! The old has gone! The new has arrived!

When Jesus is baptized by John, heaven is "opened" and the Spirit of God "descends like a dove" upon Jesus Christ. The voice of the Father then sounds from heaven: *"You are my beloved Son; in you I am well pleased."*[29] Mark's gospel account is a standout because the Greek word used to describe the opening of the heavens means to "tear" or to "rend." It is the same word used in Mark 15:38 to describe the tearing of the temple veil, which symbolically separated heaven and earth. The point is that Christ, Himself an open heaven, has destroyed the barrier and dividing wall between heaven and earth, God's reality and our reality. Jesus Himself said to the disciples, *"Very truly I tell you, you will see heaven open, and the angels of God ascending and descending on the Son of Man"* (John 1:51, NIV). This Christ, this "Son of Man" is the one who now lives within us, enabling us to become the sons of God!

---

[29] This event is significant enough to be included in all four gospels. See Luke 3:21-22, Matthew 3:16-17, Mark 1:10-11 and John 1:29-33.

The parallels between Christ's baptism and Jacob's ladder are striking. In both accounts, heaven opens, the Lord speaks, and a heaven-to-earth exchange occurs. Both of these instances speak of our inheritance in Christ. We have an open heaven. We are God's sons and daughters with whom He is well pleased. The Holy Spirit facilitates our interaction with heaven. Christ, the new temple, now lives within us, enabling us to join Him as a newly formed spiritual "building" that God intends to use as a home base in His mission to transform the entire world.

We live in this "vertical" spiritual relationship with the Father so that we may disperse His blessings "horizontally" in our natural environments and experiences. This simultaneous relationship with heaven and earth is symbolized in the traditional figure of the cross. A cross has vertical and horizontal wooden posts that come together at a fixed point. We can imagine that Jesus hung in the center of the cross at this fixed point of contact. He was the new temple, the meeting place of two realms. Having been drawn up into Christ, we now have the opportunity to live in this reality. The new humanity is this fixed point of contact where the realities of heaven meet earth.

The Nature of Miracles

An open heaven gives us access to God's realm. Let's return to the analogy of the spiritual toolbelt. As God's elect missionary community to a dark and unbelieving world, we must not limit ourselves to one, two, or three spiritual tools that we hope will draw people to Christ. We need a full toolbelt. Knowledge and intellectual arguments about God carry less and less weight in a postmodern culture where the concept of truth is becoming increasingly vague. This is where "miracles" - tangible manifestations of God's presence- become an essential component of our missional calling.

Today, it is so easy both inside and outside of the Church to misunderstand the concept of a miracle. A miracle is traditionally understood as an inexplicable, extraordinary event that defies scientific laws and points to a higher reality. However, the main purpose of miracles in the Bible is not to somehow authenticate or validate the ministry of Jesus and the apostles by extraordinary means. They weren't "proofs" of Jesus' divinity that the world needed to see in order to believe. Instead, miracles were a sign that the kingdom of heaven had come to earth in and through the person of Christ.

Signs and wonders invite us to see in the natural the spiritual realities of the now-present kingdom of God. Miracles reveal the nature of Christ and His mission.

As the Word of God, Jesus Christ is the Creator and Sustainer of the universe. He *is* the embodiment of the laws of the cosmos. The miracles He performed (changing water into wine, calming storms, raising the dead, healing people, multiplying food, etc.) were not really extraordinary events. They were simply His reality. His miracles invited those around Him into a tangible experience of God's realm, accessible through faith and trust. God's reality is actually far more real than what we perceive as our reality.

We must understand that "miracles" happen around us every single day, but we have become grossly desensitized to this fact. The natural creation order is a sign and a wonder. Human childbirth is a miracle. Countless miracles fill our everyday lives. Science is what helps us to understand and grasp the miracles that are already present. As we grow in faith - intuitive, experiential faith - our spiritual eyes open to see God's intimate involvement in every moment of our lives. Our awareness and recognition of the miraculous increases as our faith increases. We move from reliance on pure human reason (the wisdom of the world) to reliance on the mind of Christ (the wisdom of God.)

Miracles affirm (not confirm) the *present* reality of salvation, the kingdom, and the overflowing grace of God. They *testify*. To testify is to bear witness to. Jesus did not need to perform miracles to accomplish His mission on earth or to prove Himself as the only begotten son of God. His miracles were a testimony to the greater reality of God's presence, now in the midst of the people on earth (*"the kingdom of heaven is in your midst!"* Jesus says in Luke 17:21). Miracles are a revelation of a reality: in Christ, sin has been cancelled and there is no longer a separation between God's realm and our realm. He has entered heaven and "opened" it to us on our behalf. Miracles testify to salvation and God's grace. They "reveal" the glory of a realm that now stands side-by-side with ours.

> "How shall we escape if we ignore so great a salvation? This salvation, which was first announced by the Lord, was confirmed to us by those who heard him. God also testified to it by signs, wonders and various miracles, and by gifts of the Holy Spirit distributed according to his will." Hebrews 2:3-4 (NIV)

> "What Jesus did here in Cana of Galilee was the first of the signs through which he revealed his glory, and his disciples believed in him." John 2:11 (NIV)

> "But the Jews who disbelieved stirred up the minds of the Gentiles and embittered them against the brethren. Therefore they spent a long time there speaking boldly with reliance upon the Lord, who was testifying to the word of His grace, granting that signs and wonders be done by their hands." Acts 14:2-3 (NASB)

Miracles may be loosely categorized into two types: those wrought by God alone and those wrought by God through human agents. Most, if not all, will agree that God has the potential to do anything, anywhere, at any time. There is no question about the miracles performed by God Himself in both the Old and New Testaments, of which the greatest is the resurrection of Christ. However, red flags are raised in religionist minds when miracles become associated with human agents.

Does God need humans to perform miracles? Of course, the "correct" theological answer is no. So why did (and do) miracles happen through the means of human vessels? The answer is that miracles done through humans serve to reveal and re-create the nature of Christ. How? A miracle, in essence, is the partnering of the divine will with the human will in order to accomplish a change for the kingdom in the natural realm. Thus, Jesus is the greatest miracle of all time because He is both fully God and fully man. Two natures - that of the divine and that of the human - unite in Him and become one.

Peter writes that we have become *"partakers of the divine nature"* (2 Peter 1:4). When a human enacts (participates with God in) a miracle, Christ is revealed, because God's divine power flows through human nature and influences the natural realm. The result is a manifestation in the natural realm of a spiritual reality in the kingdom of heaven. Miracles done by men have both a divine nature and a human nature. The impulse of the divine will meets the partnership of man's will. It pleases God to involve us in miracles because their two-in-one nature ultimately points to His Son, who is two natures in one. Through miracles, God displays His love for and solidarity with humanity.

The idea that God wants to use humans to accomplish miracles today is wildly offensive to many religionists (people zealously addicted to man-made ideologies about God). Yet, this idea is clearly supported by the Bible. Throughout history, God has used ordinary men and women to accomplish His extraordinary purposes on earth. The disciples and apostles were not gifted with a temporary endowment of power to somehow "prove" the deity of Jesus and the truth of the Christian "religion" (which had not even formed yet!). Miracles were an overflow of the kingdom! Heaven, God's reality, had already begun to break through the old creation order of darkness, sin, and death. They were a testimony of a greater reality that had begun to make itself known through the person and work of Jesus Christ. Jesus is the same yesterday, today, and forever. We have the same Holy Spirit that the disciples and apostles had. What is different today is the quality of our faith.

Miracles do not in and of themselves lead anyone to belief. Rather, they are an experiential invitation into a relationship with the living God, who is in all and through all things. Miracles do not prove the gospel message, nor are they exclusive to Christianity. They have been seen, heard, and recorded in many different faiths and spiritualities throughout the centuries. For example, the Jewish exorcists in Jesus' time were able to cast out demons, prophesy in God's name and perform miracles, yet Jesus rebuked them because they had no true relationship with the living God.[30] These exorcists were able to access and manifest the realities of the spiritual world, but an authentic personal relationship with God was non-existent.

God's prophetic people are called to tap into the miraculous in order to meet the challenges and needs of the times we live in. When sin and darkness

---

[30] "Many will say to me on that day, 'Lord, Lord, did we not prophesy in your name and in your name drive out demons and in your name perform many miracles?' Then I will tell them plainly, 'I never knew you. Away from me, you evildoers!'" Matthew 7:22-23 (NIV)

increase, grace (our tangible access to God's presence) increases all the more. We live in an age of miracles. God is increasing our ability to access and manifest the realities of heaven in order to radiate the light and love of His Son into the earth. A generation hungry for spiritual truth needs to see a Church that lives in and manifests an experience of God. Religious ideologies and platitudes are useless unless their application can truly and dramatically change lives. Our theology is a divine servant that must lead us into God's greater reality. If it doesn't, it is useless.

Miracles need not be extraordinary or uncommon. For God, they are normal, and they should be for us as well. In Christ, we live in a greater reality - His! The eyes of our heart have become fixed on unseen realities. Miracles overflow when we live life in true intimacy with Christ. They are a fruit of faith that is not merely logical and intellectual, but experiential and intuitive. As authentic faith grows, so does the presence of the miraculous in our lives. Authentic faith is faith built not on arguments and facts, but an experience of a Person.

Miracles are manifestations of God's presence in and amongst His new temple. I could write an entire book on manifestations of the Spirit, but what is important to understand for now is that they can be a reality for every believer. There is diversity in the body of Christ, yes, but God sets no limits on what we are able to access as individuals. He has given us everything. The ultimate purpose of our access is to edify the Body of Christ and express His nature inside and outside of the Church.

> "Now about the graces of the Spirit, brothers and sisters, I do not want you to be uninformed...Now to each one the manifestation of the Spirit is given for the common good. To one there is given through the Spirit a message of wisdom, to another a message of knowledge by means of the same Spirit, to another faith by the same Spirit, to another gifts of healing by that one Spirit, to another miraculous powers, to another prophecy, to another distinguishing between spirits, to another speaking in different kinds of tongues, and to still another the interpretation of tongues. All these are the work of one and the same Spirit, and he

> distributes them to each one, just as he determines." 1 Corinthians 12:1,7-11 (NIV)

This is one passage from the scriptures that testifies of the manifestations of the Holy Spirit. It was not intended as an exhaustive list and should not be read as such. In this passage, Paul makes the point that God's tangible presence indeed works in and manifests amongst the Christians. However, this incredible reality should not serve to puff up the pride of anyone in God's newly formed spiritual family. Love is still the ultimate goal for God's people. Miracles are a tangible way in which God expresses His love for His people. This is why Paul wrote, "the manifestation of the Spirit is given for the common good." The "common good" is the building up of the kingdom of God, which ultimately comes from faith expressing itself in love.[31]

Releasing the Word

We release heaven's realities by attuning our human will to the will of the divine Father. This is not just applying learned intellectual truths about God to our lives. It is about thinking in line with Jesus and renewing our thinking patterns to match His.

> "Therefore, I urge you, brothers and sisters, in view of God's mercy, to offer your bodies as a living sacrifice, holy and pleasing to God - this is your true and proper worship. Do not conform to the pattern of this world, but **be transformed by the renewing of your mind. Then you will be able to test and approve what God's will is** - his good, pleasing and perfect will." Romans 12:1-2 (NIV)

Renewing the mind is its own topic and my first book, *The Mind of Christ: Christian Identity in the New Creation*, is a journey into this process. Prophetic people with renewed minds are not simply interested in *what* to think about God, but *how* to think like Him. We share God's heart and mind. Remember, prophets identify with Christ in this way. Our open heaven makes it possible for the Word of God to "come" to us in the same manner that it came to the

---

[31] "The only thing that counts is faith expressing itself through love." Galatians 5:6 (NIV)

Old Testament prophets. This makes us capable of hearing and releasing what the Father is spontaneously thinking and saying over any given situation.

In the scriptures, God promises to fulfill the words of His messengers. *"I am the Lord, the Maker of all things...who carries out the words of His servants and fulfills the words of His messengers,"* God tells Isaiah the prophet (Isaiah 44:24-26, NIV). When the Word came to the prophets in the Bible, God usually asked for a subsequent action to release what was spoken over them. Let's look at some examples of this from the scriptures.

In Isaiah, an instruction to speak follows the coming of the Word:

> "'Then the word of the Lord came to Isaiah: "Go and tell Hezekiah, 'This is what the Lord, the God of your Father David, says: I have heard your prayer and seen your tears; I will add fifteen years to your life. And I will deliver you and this city from the hand of the king of Assyria. I will defend this city.'" Isaiah 38:4-6 (NIV)

There are many instances in Ezekiel where the Lord requests a "gesture" to accompany a prophetic message:

> "'Now, son of man, take a block of clay, put it in front of you and draw the city of Jerusalem on it. Then lay siege against it: Erect siege works against it, build a ramp up to it, set up camps against it and put battering rams around it...this will be a sign to the people of Israel. Then lie on your left side and put the sin of the people of Israel upon yourself.'" Ezekiel 4:1-4 (NIV)

> "The hand of the Lord was on me, and he brought me out by the Spirit of the Lord and set me in the middle of the valley; it was full of bones. He led me back and forth among them, and I saw a great many bones on the floor of the valley, bones that were very dry. He asked me, 'Son of man, can these bones live?' I said, 'Sovereign Lord, you alone know.' Then he said to me, 'Prophesy to these bones and

say to them, 'Dry bones, hear the word of the Lord! This is what the Sovereign Lord says to these bones: I will make breath enter you, and you will come to life. I will attach tendons to you and make flesh come upon you and cover you with skin; I will put breath in you, and you will come to life. Then you will know that I am the Lord.'" Ezekiel 37:1-6 (NIV)

In the story of the Valley of Dry Bones, we can see that Ezekiel's obedience to the Lord's Word was not without results. The Spirit ushered in life and power as a response to Ezekiel's obedience:

"So I prophesied as I was commanded. And as I was prophesying, there was a noise, a rattling sound, and the bones came together, bone to bone." Ezekiel 37:7 (NIV)

Here in Ezekiel 37, we can see clearly a certain *prophetic formula*. First, there is the coming of the Word of God, then a human action, and finally God's reaction to the human action.

What about examples from the New Testament? There are both explicit and implicit examples. An explicit example would be Peter's famous walk on the water. When the Lord calls to Him, He doesn't stay in the boat. He gets out and starts walking on the water. Peter's act of obedience is what activates the Lord's power. There was a call and a human action required by Peter that partnered His will with the will of the Lord. The human met the Divine to produce a "supernatural" reality.[32]

An implicit example would be the life of Paul. Paul was just one man, one yielded life. His steadfast obedience in following the voice of the Holy Spirit changed the entire world. Paul lived in absolute obedience to the voice of the One who loved him. His human will was enthralled by the love of the Divine will.

These are just a few examples of prophetic action from the scriptures but we can see a theme starting to emerge: obedience in our realm to the Word of

---

[32] For this story, see Matthew 14.

the Lord releases the realities of heaven. Of course, our obedience is dependent on both our ability to hear God's voice and our faith (trust) in carrying out what we believe He is saying. This is where spiritual maturity and bravery come into play. We learn His voice by spending quality time with Him in prayer, meditation, and worship. There is no other way. The mind of Christ does not come overnight. It grows like a tree, slowly yet surely, and bears its fruit in proper season. Once we begin to taste this fruit, the prophetic lifestyle becomes addicting. We earnestly desire more.

I think most Christians would agree that God still speaks today. However, there is often disagreement on the way that this happens. It is important to understand that the Bible is not God. The pages and the ink mean absolutely nothing. What matters is the voice of the Holy Spirit, who speaks through the written Word of God, enabling us to encounter the living Christ. The Bible is not the center of all Christian life - fellowship with Christ and each other through the Spirit is. The scriptures are a collection of prophetic writings that invite us into a timeless experience of God's love. The literal words do not transform us, but the spiritual presence that accompanies the words does. God has given us the Bible because we would be utterly helpless without it. It is an aid, a tool. It is a map that leads us to a destination. The idea is that when we ultimately reach the destination, the map can be set aside. This is what it will be like at the full consummation of God's kingdom. The Bible will be set aside, because humanity will be living in the fullest experience and revelation of God's holy and personal presence.

Religious fear prevents us from abandoning faulty and dated understandings of the Bible, which has already been subject to so much perversion, misunderstanding, and abuse throughout the centuries. The reality of Christianity is that God has already given us all of Himself. Our inner fears and religious arrogance prevent us from experiencing this fullness. The kingdom of heaven is fully within us. Yet, at the same time, there is a tension between who we are and who we may be.

The New Testament scriptures clearly teach that the "Word" of God now lives within us. This eternal life, this divinity, now flows through our imperfect humanity. The apostle Paul puts it like this:

> "For God, who said, 'Let light shine out of darkness,' made his light shine in our hearts to give us the light of the knowledge of God's glory displayed in the face of Christ. But we have this treasure in jars of clay to show that this all-surpassing power is from God and not from us." 2 Corinthians 4:6-7 (NIV)

This is the tension of Christian identity. As the new temple of God, we are in union with Christ and have been brought into His fullness. However, we must grapple with the fact that at the end of the day we are still human. We have not achieved full divinity or the glory of a heavenly body. We war against sin, darkness, and decay in our earthly form. We carry in our bodies the "death of Jesus" so that His life may be revealed in us and through us. We have the mind of Christ, yet the passions of the old creation strive to re-assert themselves. It can be maddening but there is a strange beauty here. God is using imperfect humanity to achieve something that, in the end, will be quite perfect.

As we learn to steward God's presence and identify with God's heart, we move into a deeper experience of His presence and power. He "gives us the kingdom."[33] We move from fear to faith, from a kingdom that is "not yet" to a kingdom that is fully "at hand." We are already the children of God, and what we will be has not yet been made known. But we know that when Christ appears, we shall be like Him, for we shall see Him as He is.[34] Indeed, the light of the glory of Christ is already shining! We must fully awaken to this reality.

> "Arise, shine, for your light has come, and the glory of the Lord rises upon you. See, darkness covers the earth and thick darkness is over the peoples, but the Lord rises upon you and his glory appears over you. Nations will come to

---

[33] "Do not be afraid, little flock, for your Father has been pleased to give you the kingdom." Luke 12:32 (NIV)

[34] "Beloved, now we are children of God, and it has not appeared as yet what we will be. We know that when He appears, we will be like Him, because we will see Him just as He is." 1 John 3:2 (NIV)

> your light and kings to the brightness of your dawn." Isaiah 60:1-3 (NIV)

> "The people living in darkness have seen a great light; on those living in the land of the shadow of death a light has dawned...From that time on Jesus began to preach, 'Repent, for the kingdom of heaven has come near.'" Matthew 4:16-17 (NIV)

> "Wake up sleeper, rise from the dead, and Christ will shine on you." Ephesians 5:14 (NIV)

God's prophetic people radiate the glory that is already at hand. They see the sun that is rising and beginning to shine over all of humanity. They are captivated by the beauty of Christ's Second Coming and invite others to see the shimmering light of Truth that already streaks across time's horizon.[35]

Hearing God's Voice

God's prophetic people must grow in learning how to hear and respond to God's voice. I believe that this is essential for Christian faith in the 21st century and beyond. You may be thinking, "This sounds good, but how can I know if I am hearing God's voice? How do I differentiate my thoughts from God's?"

Hearing God's voice is actually far less complicated than we make it out to be. All Christians have been given the Holy Spirit, who allows us to directly connect to what the Father is saying and doing. It is a matter of simply believing and trusting that we can.

Open heavens, miracles, and gifts of the Spirit are impossible without the constant flow of heaven through our minds. Jesus said, *"Man does not live on bread alone, but on every word that comes from the mouth of God"* (Matthew 4:4, NIV). Hearing from God is the spiritual sustenance of prophets - our daily bread.

---

[35] "Yet I am writing you a new command; its truth is seen in him and in you, because the darkness is passing and the true light is already shining." 1 John 2:8 (NIV)

"Word" here in Matthew 4:4 is the Greek *rhema*, which is the spoken, living word of God for the present moment. Prophets live in a flow of God's *rhema*.

This is made possible through the prophetic anointing. The anointing gives us direct access to God, as we have already thoroughly established. We are able to interact and communicate with God as a personal being. Jesus said, *"My sheep listen to my voice; I know them, and they follow me"* (John 10:27, NIV). His presence is active in and amongst us. He guides us and teaches us in all things.

Learning the "language" of the Spirit is not hard, but it requires belief and a little bit of practice. God speaks to each of us in a unique way. I experience the voice of God as a specific "channel" in my mind. There are thoughts in my head that have a certain quality and feel to them that I am able to recognize as the Spirit of Christ. As we develop a genuine relationship with God that extends beyond mere knowledge, it becomes easier and easier to differentiate the voice of the Holy Spirit from other voices.

A commonly believed myth in Christianity today is that access to God's voice is reserved for certain "gifted" people. The truth is that God is always speaking to everyone, even non-believers, but our minds must become attuned to His channel. He has always been speaking, is speaking, and will always be speaking with His children, even to those who are far from His heart.

Just as if it were a natural language, the language of the Spirit takes time, patience, and practice. It requires trust, risk, and community. I believe God is more eager for us to hear His voice than we are to listen for it. What, if anything, can be done on our end to accelerate our ability to hear from and release heaven?

1. Openness. If our hearts are not open to the idea of God speaking with His human sons and daughters, we will not be able to hear His voice. Simple child-like belief facilitates a deeper experience of God.

2. Time in God's presence. We live in an age of distraction. This only makes the spiritual path harder, but God has given more grace. Time with God, be it in prayer, meditation, reading, or worship, grows our sensitivity to His presence. This is where we can see the incredible grace God has given to us through the Bible. The Bible facilitates a living relationship with Christ. When we read the Bible, the perceived veil between heaven and earth thins. The anointed words penetrate our hearts and minds and propel us into the atmosphere of heaven. When we attune our minds to Him, God brings His presence.

3. Practicing stillness and silence. God urges the Psalmist, *"Be still and know that I am God"* (Psalm 46:10, NIV). We must grow in our ability to rest - to become still both physically and spiritually. This is difficult in an age of noise. God speaks most often in the "still small voice." Practice sitting in stillness and take self- inventory. Are you restless? Is stillness difficult for you? Invite God's presence to envelope your heart and mind. Contemplate and reflect on your thoughts. Are you noticing any thoughts in particular? Do you see anything in your imagination? It is the unrenewed mind that wants to tell you that what you see or hear is "just you." Ask God what He is saying and speaking to you and allow the inner dialogue to develop. Ask the Holy Spirit specific questions about what you are hearing or seeing in your mind's eye. A purified imagination is the Holy Spirit's playground.

If you can practice these three core elements - openness, time in God's presence, and the discipline of stillness - you will be hearing and discerning your personal "God channel" in no time. It is not difficult. I do not speak as an expert or one who has "arrived," but as someone who is constantly learning. I have found the biggest impediments in my spiritual practice to be feelings of unworthiness, a busy mind, or an inability to truly be still. Do not allow shame or accusation a place in your conversations with God. We must be patient in learning. Focused time with God can start as a few minutes a day. This is enough. Make it a habit. As you do, the door of spiritual discernment will open for you.

The apostle John advises God's prophetic people to "test the spirits":

> "Dear friends, do not believe every spirit, but test the spirits to see whether they are from God, because many false prophets have gone out into the world. This is how you can recognize the Spirit of God: Every spirit that acknowledges that Jesus Christ has come in the flesh is from God, but

every spirit that does not acknowledge Jesus is not from God…" 1 John 4:1-3 (NIV)

God's voice will always be aligned to the fruit of the Spirit - love, joy, peace, patience, kindness, goodness, faithfulness, gentleness, and self-control. God will never encourage us to do something that is not in line with the character or spirit of Jesus Christ. Part of "acknowledging" Jesus Christ is aligning with His character. For example, God's Spirit would never fill our minds with hopeless thoughts or invite us to speak degrading words over another person.

Risk and Reward

In hearing God's voice, we must allow our trust in Jesus to override our fear of spiritual deception. This is where faith comes into play. Fear prevents us from living in the fullness of Christ's inheritance. We are God's prophetic people, His anointed sons and daughters, who have been hidden in Christ.[36] He promises to protect us as we explore a deeper, more tangible experience of His person.

Hearing God requires an element of risk. Our ability to hear the Holy Spirit will not mature if we do not take risks to follow what we think we are hearing from God. If you hear what you think is God speaking over a certain situation, take action. As we have learned, this is what releases His grace and power. God teaches us through experience as we risk and trust in Him. This is where the rubber hits the road in the Christian lifestyle. Faith is *doing*. We cannot grow and learn if we are not willing to risk.

As we mature in the anointing and attune ourselves to the mind of Christ and the heart of the Father, we will find Him initiating conversation with us more frequently. He sends divine impulses so that we may share prophetic words or release graces over people. Our ability to tune in to what He is doing and saying at all times grows as we fall deeper in love with Him. The Father trusts us with so much.

---

[36] "For you died, and your life is now hidden with Christ in God." Colossians 3:3 (NIV)

I would like to share a personal example of the prophetic anointing in action. I was recently on a missions trip to Croatia with a group of Christians who were very open to the prophetic. We spent time walking the streets in the country's capital of Zagreb. We were using this time as an opportunity to practice hearing from the Lord. Our hope was that some Croatians would in some way be impacted by the love of the Father.

One afternoon, we were walking through the center of the city and I noticed a woman sitting hunched under a streetlight with a basket out in front of her. I approached her with a translator and began speaking with her. She would not look at me. When I asked her to tell me a little about herself, she looked up. I could immediately see that half of her face was horribly disfigured. She shared with us that she had had several surgeries in her youth to correct a major problem with her eyes, but the doctors ended up doing more harm than good. She had been left permanently blind in her right eye with partial disfigurement of the face.

I wasn't really sure what to do so I checked in with the Holy Spirit. I wanted to know what the Father was doing or saying. To my shock, I heard the Holy Spirit say, "put spit on her eyes." I hesitated. *No, that can't be God*, I thought. *Too weird. Too unusual. Didn't Jesus do something like that? I certainly am not Jesus.*

We continued making basic conversation. Some others from the group came over to talk to her and give some money. I offered her a couple of generic Christianese lines like "God loves you" and "God has a plan for you." These words didn't seem to mean much to her. Later, I realized this was not what the Father was trying to say to her in the moment. As we were preparing to leave, I couldn't ignore the burning internal impression that I was actually supposed to put spit on this woman's eyes. I took a deep breath and turned towards her.

"This sounds a little crazy, but I feel that God wants me to put spit on your eyes. Would you trust me with that?" I asked.

To my complete shock, she nodded her head and said, "I trust you" without any hesitation.

My companions grinned sheepishly as I spit into my hand, took a nervous gulp, and put my fingers directly into her eyes. We waited a moment. Nothing seemed to happen. My stomach dropped and I began to think of how ridiculously insane this must seem to everyone around us. Suddenly, the women began gasping. She told us a bright light was appearing in her blind eye. To be honest, I was shocked. I then felt we were supposed to continue praying, so we did so. Tears began to run down her cheeks as she told us the light was getting brighter and an intense, unusual heat was filling her entire body. She told us she couldn't explain what was happening, but she knew God was doing something. We were all stunned by this turn of events. At this point, I was expecting a full physical healing, but it never happened. She wasn't regaining sight in her eye, which left me a little disappointed. However, she wouldn't stop talking about the light and warmth in her paralyzed eye. After a few more minutes of praying and encouraging her, I felt it was time to move on.

I have no idea if that woman's eye was ever fully healed. What I do know is that I was indeed hearing from the Lord and my act of obedience prompted some sort of manifestation in the natural realm. She told us that no one had ever paid attention to her the way we had. This woman felt the tangible love of God, probably for the first time in her life. My obedience to what I felt God saying released His presence and power over her mind, body, and heart. Who knows what God did in her life after we left her? We did not see her on the streets again.

I share this story because it offers an example of how the prophetic anointing operates. The Word of God comes to us through impressions, mental images, and thoughts. God invites us to respond by taking action. This allows God to release His power through us and radiate His love and kindness into the world. This spirituality and lifestyle paradigm are for everyone, not just a few "gifted" people. As we push against fear and take risks, we will begin to see God using us, ordinary people, in extraordinary ways.

***

In this chapter, we explored our heavenly mandate to release God's presence. God's prophetic people have an open heaven, which gives us full access to the graces and gifts of the heavenly realm. Our ability to align and partner with the divine will reveals the character and nature of Jesus Christ. We release the presence of the Lord into our environments and situations by acting in obedience to what we feel He is saying. We grow in our ability to hear God's voice by spending time in His presence - be it in worship, prayer, meditation, or study of the scriptures. Our potential to operate in the gifts of the Spirit is predicated on our ability to trust God and step out in faith. As we move from fear to faith, God's tangible presence in our lives becomes more and more pervasive.

This concludes our exploration of the prophetic dimension of the anointing of the Holy Spirit. Christians are "Christ-ones," God's anointed sons and daughters who have been given direct access to His presence. We carry the presence of God, identify with God's heart and mind, and release the power of God. We were once "dead" and separated from God because of sin. In Christ, we have been made alive. As carriers of God's eternal life, we are now "sons of humanity" - living signs and symbols of what humanity as a whole will one day become. Like Jesus, we are called to live in a flow of what the Father is saying and doing in the present moment.

Our union with Christ empowers us to live just like He did. God does not give us access to the powers of the age to come merely for our own benefit. Our mission is to radiate His light into the spiritual darkness that shrouds humanity. Miracles and the graces of the Holy Spirit do not serve to confirm some sort of intellectual gospel message but *affirm* that the kingdom of God is already at hand. We live between the ages - between what has already been made known and what will soon be in regard to the kingdom of God. The prophetic anointing is an incredible and sometimes unbelievable responsibility that the Lord has given us to steward. As we grow in this gift and radiate His light, the nations will run to the brightness of the Lord's dawn.

We will end this chapter with a promise from the Lord to His prophetic people:

> "While Jeremiah was still confined in the courtyard of the guard, the word of the Lord came to him a second time: 'This is what the Lord says, he who made the earth, the Lord who formed it and established it - the Lord is his name:

'Call to me and I will answer you and tell you great and unsearchable things you do not know.'" Jeremiah 33:1-3 (NIV)

If we call, the Lord promises to answer. The Word of God will come to us. Let us be brave and bold to call out for the great and unsearchable things God has prepared for us and others. It is this boldness before God and man that will manifest God's will, on earth as it is in heaven.

Part Two

Priests

❝*You are a chosen people, a royal priesthood, a holy nation, God's special possession, that you may declare the praises of him who called you out of darkness into his wonderful light.*" The apostle Peter wrote these incredible words nearly two thousand years ago. *Chosen. Royal. A holy nation.* Peculiar words to describe a group of "depraved sinners!" He continues, "*Once you were not a people, but now you are the people of God*" (1 Peter 2:9-10, NIV). Perhaps Peter had in mind the words of Paul, who had written the following to the Ephesians just a few years earlier:

> "As for you, you were dead in your transgressions and sins ("Once you were not a people"), in which you used to live when you followed the ways of this world...we were by nature deserving of wrath. But because of his great love for us, God, who is rich in mercy, made us alive with Christ even when we were dead in transgressions - it is by grace you have been saved. And God raised us up with Christ and seated us with him in the heavenly realms in Christ Jesus ("but now you are the people of God") ..." Ephesians 2:1-6 (NIV), parenthetical annotations from 1 Peter 2:9-10

Peter's words introduce us to the second spiritual office bestowed upon us by the anointing: the office of spiritual priesthood. As God's anointed new humanity, we constitute a "kingdom," a global family of spiritual priests. This is an extremely powerful reality of the Christian faith that is often under-taught in the modern Church. Understanding this office and its dimensions is key for the Church to be able to live with vision, power, and effectiveness for God's purposes in the 21st century and beyond. So, what is a New Covenant priest?

A priest is an anointed individual who offers spiritual sacrifices to God through worship, fellowship, and evangelism.

All believers are priests in the currently advancing kingdom of God. We will examine how the Old Covenant priesthood foreshadowed the remarkable responsibilities now given to God's new humanity. The truths we will uncover together will challenge your existing beliefs about yourself, God's destiny for you, and the role of the Church. You will feel emboldened and empowered to embrace your identity and calling as an anointed priest of the living God.

Chapter Five

The Royal Priesthood

It is sometimes shocking to read stories about the priests of ancient Israel. God seemed to demand a lot from them: *Do this. Do that. Make sure it is perfect. Kill an animal, spill its blood, remove the guts, burn it up.* If the priests did something wrong, God struck them dead. It is all extremely off-putting and bizarre to modern sensibilities. However, if we can view these strange duties of the Old Testament priests through the lens of Jesus Christ, we will see the beautiful realities of the current kingdom of God in symbolic form.

The natural realities of the Old Testament foreshadowed the spiritual realities of the New. They were a *"shadow of the things that were to come; the reality, however, is found in Christ"* (Colossians 2:17, NIV). The Old Covenant sacrificial system was but a *"copy and a shadow of what is in heaven"* (Hebrews 8:5, NIV). It is not necessary for us to get into the details of the Old Covenant priesthood. There were a lot of rules, regulations, and requirements… and a whole lot of blood. Instead of doing an in-depth Bible study on the topic, I want to highlight what is essential and relevant for our priestly role in the new creation.

Our Great High Priest

A priest is someone who acts as a mediator between God and man. He ministers on behalf of God as His representative, His ambassador. Under the

Aaronic and Levitical priesthoods of the Old Testament, the priests offered animal sacrifices in the tabernacle and temple in order to atone (make spiritual amends) for the sins of the people. These priests were also responsible for educating the people in God's precepts, judging matters amongst the people, and facilitating worship. All of these duties were performed within the context of a complex system of worship that God had given to the Israelites during their wilderness wandering.

The high priest was the leader of the priests. He was responsible for directly entering into the Holy of Holies (the deepest part of the tabernacle/temple) to sprinkle blood on "God's throne," in order to atone for the sin of the people. This would "appease" the wrath of God. The problem with this system was that it could not ultimately free people from awareness of their sin. Awareness of sin is what causes people to act on sin. Thus, death (separation from God's presence) continued amongst the Israelite people.

The book of Hebrews tells us that Jesus is our *"great high priest, who has ascended into heaven"* on our behalf (Hebrews 4:14, NIV). Jesus, through His sacrificial death, embodied the work of the high priest. Rather than offering the blood of animals, however, He offered Himself as a sacrifice. The altar for this sacrifice was not God's throne in the temple, but a cross on a hill outside the city of Jerusalem. There, the divine God-man took the sins of the world upon Himself and brought them into the grave. This is the act that would initiate the new creation. The old order - full of sin, death and decay - went with Jesus into His death.

Paul writes the following in 2 Corinthians shortly after informing the believers that they are now part of the new creation (v.17):

> "God made [Christ] who had no sin to be sin for us, so that in him we might become the righteousness of God." 2 Corinthians 5:21 (NIV)

The righteousness of God means we are now in "right-standing" with God. There is no longer sin or sin consciousness that separates us from His presence. As we learned in Part One of this book, we now fully identify with Jesus Christ in every possible way. Jesus, through His death and resurrection, abolished the old priesthood and inaugurated something quite new. Christ, as the priest-mediator of a new partnership between God and man, forgave our sin and has given us access to the life of heaven and a spiritual inheritance.

As God's priests, we now participate in this new, superior spiritual priesthood. This is possible because we are seated with Christ in the heavenly realms. Unlike the Old Testament priests, Christ did not enter a sanctuary made with human hands but has ascended into heaven's sanctuary in order to appear for us (and as us!) in God's presence. This allows us to approach God the Father with great freedom and confidence. We are in union with Christ and have the same access to the Father that He has.

> "God raised us up with Christ and seated us with him in the heavenly realms in Christ Jesus." Ephesians 2:6 (NIV)

> "In him and through faith in him we may approach God with freedom and confidence." Ephesians 3:12 (NIV)

These powerful truths are often downplayed or misunderstood in the modern Church. We are still largely preoccupied with sin management. Our Sunday messages and Bible studies tend to focus on how to curb our depraved nature by applying "truths" from the Bible. We learn what to think about God and the Bible, not how to think like Christ. The problem with this, of course, is that it keeps us conscious of sin instead of bringing us into the revelation of freedom that characterizes the new creation. Christ's work was supposed to free us from sin consciousness, not keep us aware of and enslaved to our depravity and imperfection. Our call is not to perform for holiness, but to rest in the perfection that is found only in Christ. We died with Him and we now live with Him. The scriptures clearly teach that we have been completely purified and even "perfected" in the blood of Jesus:

> "For by one sacrifice he has made perfect forever those who are being made holy." Hebrews 10:14 (NIV)

> "Therefore, brothers and sisters, since we have confidence to enter the Most Holy Place (God's presence) by the blood of Jesus, by a new and living way (the new creation) opened to us through the curtain, that is, his body, and since we

> have a great high priest over the house of God (the Body of Christ), let us draw near to God with a sincere heart and with the full assurance that faith brings, having our hearts sprinkled to cleanse us from a guilty conscience and having our bodies washed with pure water (the mind of Christ)." Hebrews 10:19-22 (NIV), parenthetical annotations mine

As new creations, we walk "in the blood" of Jesus Christ. Our sins - past, present, and future - were done away with nearly two thousand years ago. This profound revelation spurns us to obedience. We walk in God's ways because we have been empowered to. We have been given a trust to steward Christ's presence and grow into His image. As we rest and abide in Him, we will not sin. We do not need to worry about performing for God. If there is sin, if the enemy happens to draw us off the narrow way, God is faithful to cleanse our minds and hearts so that we can continue the spiritual journey into God's heart. This is what it means to grow in holiness, which is Godlikeness.[37] He is forever for us and never against us.

Living Stones

Our union with Christ and the anointing has made us into a kingdom of priests. The book of Revelation tells us that Christ has freed us from our sins and *"made us to be a kingdom and priests to serve His God and Father"* (Revelation 1:6, NIV). We must remind ourselves that the Body of Christ is the new temple of the living God, the location of God's manifest presence on earth. The dynamic working of the Holy Spirit in and amongst us affirms this reality. This incredible new temple is not a building, but a group of humans who live in the reality of the new creation through faith in Christ. We are "living stones" that God is using to build a glorified house in which His presence can tangibly dwell.

> "As you come to him, the living Stone - rejected by humans but chosen by God and precious to him - you also, like living stones are being built into a temple of the Spirit to be a holy

---

[37] "You were taught, with regard to your former way of life, to put off your old self, which is being corrupted by its deceitful desires; to be made new in the attitude of your minds; and to put on the new self, created to be like God in true righteousness and holiness." Ephesians 4:22-24 (NIV)

priesthood, offering spiritual sacrifices acceptable to God through Jesus Christ." 1 Peter 2:4-5 (NIV)

"For through [Christ] we both have access to the Father by one Spirit. Consequently, you are no longer foreigners and strangers, but fellow citizens with God's people and also members of his household...In him the whole building is joined together and rises to become a holy temple in the Lord. And in him you too are being built together to become a dwelling in which God lives by His Spirit." Ephesians 2:18-22 (NIV)

It is crucial for us to understand that God has never intended His manifest presence to be limited to a single location. After all, the whole earth is the Lord's and everything in it.[38] God is building a global tabernacle out of the new creation priesthood. We are a spiritual temple that spreads throughout the entire earth. Believers are the "living stones" of this temple and the Holy Spirit is the cement that binds us together.

From the gospel accounts, we read that Jesus' earthly profession was that of a builder and a carpenter. Jesus' natural profession foreshadowed His spiritual destiny. The ascended Christ is at work in His people, crafting us into His mature image so that His presence in the world can become apparent and obvious. Jesus Himself is the starting point of this new temple. The scriptures call Him the "cornerstone" - the part of a building that must be laid first before everything else can follow.[39] As the first member of God's new creation, Christ is our guide, model and pattern. It is the priestly anointing that allows us to participate in God's grand temple-building project.

The Last Adam and the New Jerusalem

To better comprehend our priestly role in the new creation building project, we must examine Adam, the first man. God gave Adam a "garden" to tend and expand. In this garden, Adam walked freely in the presence of God. Adam was the very first priest in that He tended to God's garden temple and

---

[38] "The earth is the Lord's, and everything in it, the world, and all who live in it." Psalms 24:1 (NIV)

[39] See 1 Peter 2:6-8.

lived a life of worship by carrying out God's commands. Adam's mission was to "subdue" the earth and rule over the works of the Lord.

> "Then God said, 'Let us make mankind in our image, in our likeness, so that they may rule over the fish in the sea and the birds in the sky, over the livestock and all the wild animals, and over all the creatures that move along the ground...God blessed [humanity] and said to them, 'Be fruitful and increase in number; fill the earth and subdue it. Rule over the fish in the sea and the birds in the sky and over every living creature that moves on the ground.'" Genesis 1:26,28 (NIV)

Most people know what happened in the Garden. Adam compromised and sin entered into the creation order. Thus, Adam failed in the duties of his priesthood. His sin expelled him from the glory of God's sanctuary, the temple he had been called to steward. Mankind fell into darkness. However, God already had a plan of redemption and salvation in the works. The manifestation of this plan would develop slowly for thousands of years. Eventually, in God's perfect timing, Jesus Christ, the first priest of the new creation, would arrive on the scene and forever change the destiny of humanity.

The apostle Paul refers to Christ as the "last Adam" in 1 Corinthians 15:

> "So it is written: 'The first man Adam became a living being'; the last Adam (Christ), a life-giving spirit. The spiritual did not come first, but the natural, and after that the spiritual. [Adam] was of the dust of the earth; [Christ] is of heaven. As was [Adam] so are those who are of the earth; and as is [Christ], so also are those who are of heaven. And just as we have borne the image of [Adam], so let us bear the image of [Christ]. I declare to you, brothers and sisters, that flesh and blood (the old creation) cannot inherit the kingdom of God, nor does the perishable inherit the imperishable." 1 Corinthians 15:45-50 (NIV), parenthetical annotations mine

This is a crucial passage for understanding the reality of the new creation. You may need to read it a second time. Contextually, Paul is speaking about the resurrection and the reality that we will share a glorified body modeled after the resurrected Christ. But notice the clear "heaven and earth" language. Again, we must think of "heaven" not as a distant, idyllic destination, but as an ever-increasing reality that has already begun to break into our realm of experience (*"the kingdom of heaven is at hand"*). What Paul is doing is comparing and contrasting two patterns of existence: that of Adam, who was full of weakness and death, and that of Christ, who bursts with power and divine life.

Where Adam's priesthood of "flesh and blood" failed, the priesthood of Christ, the "life-giving spirit," will succeed. We bear the image of Christ, the heavenly man, and are being conformed into this image with ever-increasing glory. Adam's priesthood could not inherit the kingdom of God, but the new creation priesthood can. Christ's kingdom is the kingdom of the Holy Spirit, who lives within us.

Adam had a garden. Christ has a city. This city is known in the scriptures as the "New Jerusalem." We are priests in this city of God, whose architect and builder is Jesus Christ. The New Jerusalem is the ever-expanding global temple of God, consisting of His "living stones." We can read in the book of Revelation that the throne of God is within the New Jerusalem. In this spiritual city, the servants of God see His face, serve Him, and reign forever and ever.[40]

The biblical reality is that the Body of Christ is the New Jerusalem, a new creation temple without walls. God has given us the Spirit of Christ, which allows us to contemplate His face. The New Jerusalem is alight with the presence of God. He is enthroned on the praises of His royal priesthood.[41] It is in this "city," this new temple, that we tend to our priestly duties. The New Jerusalem is the manifestation of the kingdom of heaven. We are the bride of

---

[40] "No longer will there be any curse. The throne of God and of the Lamb will be in the city, and his servants will serve him. They will see his face, and his name will be on their foreheads. There will be no more night. They will not need the light of a lamp or the light of the sun, for the Lord God will give them light. And they will reign for ever and ever." Revelation 22:3-5 (NIV)

[41] "You are holy, enthroned on the praises of Israel." Psalms 22:3 (NIV)

Christ and the Holy Spirit represents the consummation of our union with Him.

> "Then I saw 'a new heaven and a new earth,' for the first heaven and the first earth (the old creation) had passed away and there was no longer any sea. **I saw the Holy City, the new Jerusalem**, coming down out of heaven from God, prepared as a bride beautifully dressed for her husband." Revelation 21:1-2 (NIV), parenthetical annotations mine

> "But you have come to Mount Zion, **to the city of the living God, the heavenly Jerusalem**. You have come to thousands upon thousands of angels in joyful assembly, to the church of the firstborn, whose names are written in heaven. You have come to God, the Judge of all, to the spirits of the righteous made perfect, to Jesus the mediator of a new covenant, and to the sprinkled blood that speaks a better word than the blood of Abel." Hebrews 12:22-24 (NIV)

The mandate of God's royal priesthood is to expand the kingdom of heaven, the New Jerusalem, to all corners of the globe. And how will this occur? This is where we share the duties of Adam and the Old Testament priests, but we now perform them in a spiritual manner. We offer spiritual sacrifices and worship to the living God, while building each other up through love and the gifts of the Holy Spirit. Together, we build the temple of God by increasing its depth and breadth on Planet Earth.

I envision a bustling global network of new creation humans (Christians). God's presence guides and infuses everything they do, which are the good works that God has prepared in advance for us to walk in.[42] Love is paramount to this group of people, and everything that is done is done to serve one another and God. Jesus' presence and healing power flow out of these works to a broken and lost humanity. Eventually, the nations will see

---

[42] "For we are God's handiwork, created in Christ Jesus to do good works, which God prepared in advance for us to do." Ephesians 2:10 (NIV)

this thriving global community and desire the presence of Christ for themselves. The book of Revelation tells us that these are indeed some characteristics of the New Jerusalem, God's new temple:

> "I did not see a temple in this city, because the Lord God almighty and the Lamb are its temple. The city does not need the sun or the moon to shine on it, for the glory of God gives it light, and the Lamb is its lamp. **The nations will walk by its light, and the kings of the earth will bring their splendor into it.**" Revelation 21:22-23 (NIV)

> "Then the angel showed me the river of the water of life, as clear as crystal, flowing from the throne of God and of the Lamb down the middle of the great street of the city. On each side of the river stood the tree of life, bearing twelve crops of fruit, yielding its fruit every month. **And the leaves of the tree are for the healing of the nations.**" Revelation 22:1-2 (NIV)

The river of life flows through the New Jerusalem. This "river" is the living water of the Holy Spirit, who flows in and through God's anointed royal priesthood. The "Tree of Life," which was also present with Adam in Eden, is none other than Jesus Christ, who now lives within us. His fruit is the fruit of the Spirit - love, joy, peace, patience, gentleness, kindness, goodness, faithfulness, and self-control. The "leaves which heal the nations" are the gifts and graces of the Holy Spirit and the good works that God has prepared for us to walk in.

The responsibility of God's priestly people is to steward these incredible realities. We do not need to strive to perfect holiness or righteousness before God. They have been given to us in Christ. 1 Corinthians 1:30 says, *"It is because of God that you are in Christ Jesus, who has become for us wisdom from God - that is, our righteousness, holiness and redemption."* We were once something entirely different - a humanity full of sin, death, and decay. But, in Christ, we have become something entirely state-of-the-art. We are new creations full of life, power, and purpose.

The royal priesthood operates from a revelation of God's love for us. Our mission is not to work for more holiness or righteousness. We don't read the Bible or pray to somehow become more holy or pure. Rather, as we steward what He has already given to us, our eyes open to see the fullness of what Christ has already accomplished on our behalf.

***

The scriptures tell us that we are God's "royal priesthood," His "holy nation." We follow in the pattern of Christ, who is the first priest of the new creation order. By atoning for the sins of humanity with a once-for-all sacrifice, He has entered into God's presence in heaven and actively enables us to do the same. This has allowed us to become a kingdom of priests who minister to God's presence in God's new temple, the Body of Christ.

Christians are the new location of God's manifest presence on Planet Earth. We are an ever-expanding community of new creation humans who serve as "living stones" in God's global building project. Our "Eden" is the city of the New Jerusalem, which is a powerful symbol of the new creation temple. God's eternal presence flows in, through, and out of this spiritual city that we inhabit. It is in this "city" that we perform our spiritual priestly duties and minister to God's presence.

New creation priests have been made completely pure and holy through the blood of our prototype, Jesus Christ. It is this gift of holiness that allows us to worship, fellowship, and evangelize in God's eternal presence. We will now dive deeper to explore our incredible priestly responsibilities.

Chapter Six

True Christian Worship

A central responsibility of God's anointed priesthood is to offer worship to the living God. Of course, worship of God is not exclusive to Christianity – many of the world's religions seek to worship the divine in one way or another. So, what makes Christian worship different? Aren't we all just worshiping the same God? To answer this, we must understand worship within the context of the anointing and God's new temple, the Body of Christ.

The issue is that us modern Christians tend to have a very narrow view of what worship actually is. For us, "worship" usually means going to some sort of church building and standing before a group of people on a stage who sing songs and play instruments. After "worship," there then comes a message, then communion, and so on. Eventually, we leave church and fall right back into the monotony of our weekly routines.

The problem is we have made worship something we *do* instead of something that we *are*. In the book of Romans, the apostle Paul gives the clearest definition of Christian worship:

> "Therefore, I urge you, brothers and sisters, in view of God's mercy, to **offer your bodies as a living sacrifice, holy and pleasing to God - this is your**

true and proper worship. Do not conform to the pattern of this world, but be transformed by the renewing of your mind. Then you will be able to test and approve what God's will is - his good, pleasing, and perfect will." Romans 12:1-2 (NIV)

I love this passage because it summarizes our proper response to the gospel in just a few sentences. We need to read between the lines here. Paul had in mind God's royal priesthood, His "new temple," when writing. The new temple is both the individual and corporate body of believers. The Old Covenant priests offered animal sacrifices to God but now we offer *ourselves*. This includes the totality of our humanity - body, mind, and spirit. This is Christian worship. Our worship is a response to the incredible work that Jesus Christ accomplished on our behalf - the new creation! We need not strive or perform for God's approval. We have already been declared holy and pleasing to God through Jesus. Our responsibility is to steward this reality by abiding in God's presence.

> "Therefore, since we have these promises (that we are the new temple of God and His sons and daughters), let us purify ourselves from everything that contaminates body and spirit, perfecting holiness out of reverence for God." 2 Corinthians 7:1 (NIV), parenthetical annotations mine

> "Therefore, since we are receiving a kingdom that cannot be shaken, let us be thankful, and so worship God acceptably with reverence and awe, for our God is a consuming fire." Hebrews 12:28 (NIV)

God's promises motivate us to action. Because we have been given His fullness, we respond accordingly as God's righteous sons and daughters. We "purify" ourselves by worshiping God, thus escaping the "pattern of this world." These patterns are the mental and spiritual paradigms of the old creation order that has already begun to pass away. Worship, therefore, becomes a matter of spiritual, mental, and physical purity. As we steward holiness, God perfects us into His image and we become more consciously aware of His living presence. Worship is a *lifestyle paradigm* that allows us to receive and manifest the kingdom of heaven.

Spirit and Truth

I like to think about worship as the direction of our mental energy toward a desired person, place, or thing. It is where we fix our mind's eye and direct our attention. Jesus said, *"God is spirit, and his worshipers must worship in Spirit and in truth"* (John 4:24, NIV). Worship in "Spirit and truth" is worship rooted in the unseen realm. It is ultimately a posture of the heart. The state of our heart determines our worship. Jesus was very aware of this reality. He constantly connected man's outward behavior to the motions of the heart. In Matthew 5:19, Jesus tells His disciples, *"For out of the heart come evil thoughts - murder, adultery, sexual immortality, theft, false testimony, slander."* Our inner realities produce outward manifestations.

The Greek word for worship is *proskuneo*. The root word of *proskuneo* implies the act of kissing. To worship God is to "kiss" God. How can we kiss an invisible God who is spirit? We do so by fixing our mental energy on Jesus Christ, who is the living "image" of an invisible God.

Paul writes in Colossians 1:15, *"The Son is the image of the invisible God, the firstborn over all creation."* More temple language! An "image" in an ancient temple was the physical representation of an invisible deity. Christ, who Himself assumed humanity, allows us to "see" and therefore worship God. We have an object, an image, upon which to meditate in order to become more like God. Jesus is the "image" in God's new temple, the Body of Christ. Paul puts it like this:

> "Now the Lord is the Spirit, and where the Spirit of the Lord is, there is freedom. And we all, who with unveiled faces contemplate the Lord's glory, are being transformed into his image with ever-increasing glory, which comes from the Lord, who is the Spirit." 2 Corinthians 3:17-18 (NIV)

To "contemplate the Lord's glory" is to direct our mental-spiritual energy toward Jesus Christ. As we do, He transforms our mind and heart to match His in greater and greater measure. The scriptures describe this transformation as "glory to glory." This means we progressively become more like the Lord in every possible way - we grow in Godlikeness. As we direct our mental energy toward Him, He shines through us.

I think about worship as a spiritual approach. I imagine Jesus is present with me, yet He stands at a distance. As I behold Him, He encourages me to take steps toward Him. He is radiating an indescribable light and His eyes are pure fire. With every moment that I focus my mental energy on Him, I take a step in His direction. With each step, I become progressively more consumed with His glory. Following this analogy to its end, there will come a point when I become so overwhelmed by Christ's light and fire that it becomes difficult to differentiate myself from Him. I become completely consumed by Him and become one with Him. Yet, amazingly, I retain my separate substance. He remains God and I remain man, but I am now participating and partaking in the splendor and glory of His divine nature.

To worship is to participate in the divine nature by directing our mental energy toward Jesus. It is less about a specific act, song, or dance, and more about a consummate lifestyle of holiness, determination, and focus. It is a spiritual "race" that we run, which will last our entire lives. The beautiful thing is that all believers - past, present, and future - run this race with us and share a common worship of Jesus.

> "Therefore, since we are surrounded by such a great cloud of witnesses, let us throw off everything that hinders and the sin that so easily entangles. And let us run with perseverance the race marked out for us, **fixing our eyes on Jesus**, the pioneer and perfecter of faith…" Hebrews 12:1-2 (NIV)

Worship is awareness of God's presence. I can worship at the grocery store, at the gym, or at a restaurant. It is a conscious direction of my mental energy toward the all-pervading presence of God. To worship is to live a lifestyle in which everything in every moment is offered back to God in gratitude and thanksgiving. As we worship God, we receive a kingdom that cannot be shaken. Our worship leads to a progressive purification of the inner man that allows God's glory to shine through us in greater and greater measure.

Cleaning House

If true worship is largely about stewarding the divine presence already within us, then spiritual, mental, and physical purity are our paramount responsibility. When I used to read passages in the New Testament regarding purity (and there are many), I used to think that I was reading instructions on what I needed to do in order to become a better Christian. I never realized that the instructions for purity laid out by the apostles were written in *response to a revelation*. The apostles realized they had already been given something. This "something" was actually more of a "someone," the Holy Spirit. The very presence of God had been poured out on "all flesh!"[43] Heaven, God's reality, had begun to manifest itself into the earthly realm! This revelation spurned a behavioral response.

What would change about our every behavior if we truly believed we had already been given access to all of God's presence, every "spiritual blessing in the heavenly realms?" We would spend so much less effort on trying to *become* something and instead rest in the reality that *we already are*. We have been made alive with Christ and sit with Him in the heavenly realms. There is nothing left on our end to accomplish. On the cross, Jesus said, "It is finished!" At the sound of these words, any distance between God's reality and ours was done away with for all time. We have been declared pure, holy, and righteous through the blood of Jesus. We are the new temple of the living God, the place where His eternal presence dwells, now and forever.

Now we can again examine the tension of Christian living we touched upon in Chapter Four. If what I have described above is true, that we already have full access to heaven, why do we not experience it? Why don't we see every Christian living in purity and righteousness, ably manifesting the kingdom of heaven in every moment? The first and most obvious answer is that we simply don't believe. The original truths of the gospel message, diluted through time, have been replaced with many theological dogmas and legalistic thinking paradigms. Over the centuries, an experiential spirituality gradually morphed into an intellectual system of religious philosophy.

Christian religionism and its proponents emphatically impress that the kingdom of heaven is mostly "not yet." Many Christian today think this way. The Christian believers of the first century, however, would most likely disagree. For them, the kingdom had come! It was already at hand! This was the source of their hope - that God had already begun to make all things new. The true light of God's fullness is already shining! What we believe, we will

---

[43] See Joel's prophecy in Joel 2:28-32.

see in our experience. This is a matter of simple psychology. The heart sees what it wants to see.

The second answer to the question I posed above is slightly more complicated. The scriptures make it clear that God's salvation occurs along three different timelines. We have *been* saved, are *being* saved, and *will be* saved. This is very confusing for Christians who consider salvation solely as a single moment (i.e. "I got saved").

It is helpful to think of salvation less as a religious ideal that determines post-life placement in "heaven" or "hell," and more of a present reality that is to be experienced. Salvation is restoration and renewal. We are being conformed into the image of Christ, from glory to glory. We have been rescued ("saved") out of the present evil age and are currently being restored and renewed ("saved") with God's eternal life. God is collectively and individually renewing our minds and hearts to match the quality of life that will be present when the kingdom of heaven is fully realized. Before the kingdom can externally manifest, it must be internally realized. This does not make heaven and hell any less of a reality, but our emphasis of understanding must be directed toward the present, not some vague and shadowy post-life existence. Thinking of the kingdom as a present reality is what motivates us to action. This understanding is what drove the New Testament writers.

As the new house of God, we are being progressively purified in our collective inner consciousness so that God's Spirit may dwell in us in all of His fullness. The thinking patterns and heart postures of the old creation order are being done away with through the working of the Holy Spirit. As the new temple of the living God, there is now no room for idolatry and devotion to the ways of the old creation order. Our worship and behavior are a response to what God has already accomplished on our behalf and continues to accomplish through us as we faithfully steward His eternal presence.

> "Since, then, you have been raised with Christ, set your hearts on things above, where Christ is, seated at the right hand of God. Set your minds above, not on earthly things. For you died, and your life is now hidden with Christ in God...Put to death, therefore, whatever belongs to your

> earthly nature: sexual immorality, impurity, lust, evil desires and greed, which is idolatry." Colossians 3:1-3,5 (NIV)

God, through the Holy Spirit, is in the process of "cleaning house." This divine house cleaning involves the destruction of our intellectual and spiritual idolatry so that the reality of God's presence may be all in all. Our God is a consuming fire. Our spiritual, religious, and mental bondages to the old creation order will go up in smoke as we yield ourselves to His glorious presence. This is what it means to offer our bodies as living sacrifices! This perspective sheds new light on Bible verses that instruct us to live in purity.

> "Do not be yoked together with unbelievers, for what do righteousness and wickedness have in common? Or what fellowship can light have with darkness?... What agreement is there between the temple of God and idols? For we are the temple of the living God...Therefore, since we have these promises, dear friends, let us purify ourselves from everything that contaminates body and spirit, perfecting holiness out of reverence for God." 2 Corinthians 6:14,16; 7:1 (NIV)

> "For the grace of God has appeared that offers salvation (restoration and renewal) to all people. It teaches us to say 'No' to ungodliness and worldly passions, and to live self-controlled, upright and godly lives in this present age, while we wait for the blessed hope - the appearing of the glory of our great God and Savior, Jesus Christ (the new creation), who gave himself for us to redeem us from all wickedness and to purify for himself a people that are his own, eager to do what is good." Titus 2:11-14 (NIV), parenthetical annotations mine

Our purity is a partnership with God. It is a loving response to what has already been accomplished. It enables Him to work within us so that we may progressively manifest the fruits of His kingdom. Our obedience in this area isn't what makes God "happy." God is already pleased with us! His Word has already declared us clean.[44] By remaining free from the sin that so easily entangles, we progress individually and corporately into the fullness of God's kingdom.

Fruits of Worship

True worship manifests in all sorts of creative expressions. One such expression is what we typically experience on Sunday morning. There is nothing wrong with flashy stage displays and ecstatic praise experiences, so long as they are grounded in the guiding direction of the Holy Spirit. One responsibility of God's New Testament priesthood is the offering of praise. Praise is an outward response to a glorious internal reality. It is not meant to be a patterned religious activity.

Concerning manifest expressions of worship, the apostle Paul writes the following:

> "Let the word of Christ (the presence of the Holy Spirit) dwell in you richly as you teach and admonish one another with all wisdom through psalms, hymns, and songs from the Spirit, singing to God with gratitude in your hearts. And whatever you do, whether in word or deed, do it all in the name of the Lord Jesus, giving thanks to God the Father through him." Colossians 3:16-17 (NIV), parenthetical annotations mine

We can notice in this passage that to worship is to do everything "in the name of the Lord Jesus." This passage indicates that anointed worship will overflow with spontaneous, Spirit-inspired psalms and hymns. For many churches today, Sunday morning worship is more of a patterned ritual than a spontaneous, Spirit-led experience. This is the fruit of dead religion that hinders fresh and revelatory experiences of God's presence. Our songs, set designs, and general church layout are usually copied from prominent, visible Christian ministries. The result is the "template effect" - churches that strive to sound and act like other churches instead of pursuing fresh, creative and individualized spiritual vision. This patterning hinders the spontaneity of the

---

[44] "You are already clean because of the word I have spoken to you." John 15:3 (NIV)

Holy Spirit and the fresh life He hopes to bring to each church. We must aim to be the people God desires us to be, not the people that other people desire us to be.

Another passage on worship from Ephesians makes an essential point in our understanding of true Christian worship:

> "Do not be foolish, but understand what the will of the Lord is. And do not get drunk with wine, for that is dissipation, but be filled with the Spirit, speaking to one another in psalms and hymns and spiritual songs, singing and making melody with your heart to the Lord; always giving thanks for all things in the name of our Lord Jesus Christ…" Ephesians 5:17-19 (NASB)

In this passage, Paul writes that the filling of the Spirit, the overflow of the anointing, will produce spontaneous expressions of worship in the Christian assembly. Paul comments that drunkenness, in contrast, is "dissipation." This is such an interesting word choice. Dissipation is the slow and gradual lapse into a state of non-being. Here, there is a beautiful contrast of life and death. Sin is dissipation and decay into a non-human state. As we are filled with the Spirit, God brings us into the fullness of our new creation humanity that has been freed from the bonds of sin and death. To worship God in the Spirit is to become fully human, to intentionally operate in the fullness of our original design. To sin is to deny God's gift of eternal life and remain in a state of death and decay.

Expressions of genuine worship extend beyond songs. Paul writes in both of these passages that whatever we do should be done "in the name of the Lord Jesus," which means all of our actions and words should be empowered by the Holy Spirit. This again reinforces the idea that "worship" is not isolated to any one particular activity. Worship is a daily spirituality that bears fruit for eternal life. To worship is to steward God's eternal presence in mind and body.

This is where the significance of art comes into the greater picture of Christian spirituality. Art manifests spiritual realities. It takes unseen spiritual realties and makes them manifest. Painting, dancing, writing of all kinds, crafting, and film are all examples of how spiritual realities can be made manifest in our natural reality. Again, remember that heaven, God's reality, is not "out there somewhere." His reality exists side-by-side with ours. Christian art is a way of expressing this reality. This is how we can be profoundly moved or even healed by a song, poem, dance, or film. The Holy Spirit uses the sounds, words, and sights as a "channel" into the natural realm.

Art is a channel for the unseen realm. This is where the concept of "inspiration" comes from. Inspiration literally means to "breathe in." Something that is inspired is "breathed in" from another realm. Inspiration is not limited to the heavenly - to what is noble, pure, and lovely. Art birthed in spiritual darkness will carry a spirit of darkness. This is why it is so important for Christians to consider spiritual "diet" - what we regularly expose ourselves to and ingest. Our worship is where we fix our attention and mental concentration. If we worship darkness, we will become like darkness. My goal here is not to instill fear or religious legalism, but we should carefully discern the forces operating behind what we expose ourselves to. We want to be careful that we do not become conscious, willful participants with the demonic realm, which is characterized by fear, hatred, division, lust, and violence.

Made in God's image, humans are living and breathing expressions of worship. Ephesians 2:10 says that we are God's *"artwork, created in Christ Jesus to do good works."* These "good works" are the myriad expressions of worship that we are capable of as partakers of the divine nature. Like our Father, we have the ability to create, to manifest tangible things that find their essential origin in the Spirit. Our outward activity is the fruit of our inner worship. Our task is to externally manifest the kingdom of heaven and God's reality. This reality is true, noble, right, pure, lovely, admirable, excellent, and praiseworthy.[45]

Jesus told His disciples, *"The Spirit gives life; the flesh counts for nothing. The words I have spoken to you - they are full of the Spirit and life"* (John 6:63, NIV). The implication here is that spiritual power accompanies and flows through

---

[45] "Finally, brothers and sisters, whatever is true, whatever is noble, whatever is right, whatever is pure, whatever is lovely, whatever is admirable – if anything is excellent or praiseworthy – think about such things." Philippians 4:8 (NIV)

natural words. Words are containers for spiritual things. This is exactly why the scriptures are so powerful. The words themselves are merely human but they carry a divine power. They are divinity garbed in humanity. Therefore, the Bible is God's artwork, a tangible manifestation of His reality. It is a masterpiece of heavenly worship.

Pray Without Ceasing

Prayer is an incredibly powerful manifestation of worship. We will always consider prayer as boring, stuffy, and ineffective unless we examine it in the light of the new creation. I myself struggled with prayer for many years. I didn't get it. I used to shame myself for not praying enough or as "powerfully" as others. It took a radical revelation for me to realize I didn't like prayer because I was approaching it from the perspective of the old creation. Much can be said of prayer and different types of prayer. I want to focus on what is relevant for our present topic: worship in the new creation.

Prayer is worship because it is communion with the Creator. Prayer is designed to manifest God's will, desire, and purpose on the earth. It is less of a ritualistic, religious act and more of a concentrated inner focus. In true prayer, words mean nothing, and the overflow of the heart means everything. It is about spiritual *alignment* - linking our spirit with the Holy Spirit in order to manifest God's reality.

So many of our personal and corporate prayers are filled with vain repetitions, empty words, and powerless supplications. This empty religious activity is rooted in a fundamental misunderstanding of Christian identity. Prayer is not an attempt to move the stone heart of a distant deity in the hopes that He will intervene on our behalf. This is the prayer of paganism. Christian prayer is of an entirely different nature.

As righteous sons and daughters of God, we have direct access to the king of the universe, who is actively working to accomplish His purposes on earth. He never turns a blind eye to our problems, situations, or circumstances. He never leaves us or forsakes us. Jesus said, *"My Father is always working, and I too am working"* (John 5:17, NIV). He is present in every moment. Worshipful prayer is learning how to recognize and respond to what the Father is *already* doing in the unseen. Our prayers are an *agreement* with the movements of heaven in order to manifest the will of the Father.

Powerful prayers that tap into the heart and mind of the Father are raw, spontaneous, and Spirit-inspired. They are not copied from a template, a prayer book, or our favorite Christian minister. They are not contrived. Mighty prayers are directed by the inner voice of the Holy Spirit, who is our channel to God's throne room. We cannot pray in accordance with what the Father is saying and doing if we have not learned how to discern His voice. This is where worship comes into play. Authentic worship releases powerful and effective prayers. It is our connection to God's voice that enables us to release His presence and power into the natural realm.

New creation prayers are rooted in our identity as God's righteous sons and daughters. James tells us that *"the prayer of a righteous person is powerful and effective"* (James 5:16, NIV). This is an objective reality. We don't need to pray harder, faster, or louder in order to get God to do something. We must rest and respond to the power that is already present in and amongst God's new temple. This requires a willing heart and an ability to listen. Spiritual listening is a difficult skill in our age of noise and energy. It requires effort, concentration, and spiritual practice. Powerful prayers are those birthed in spiritual stillness.

True prayer is focused, concentrated communion on the presence of God. This communion thrives in spiritual silence. This is why Jesus said, *"But when you pray, go into your room, close the door and pray to your Father, who is unseen. Then your Father, who sees what is done in secret, will reward you. And when you pray, do not keep on babbling like the pagans, for they think they will be heard because of their many words"* (Matthew 6:6-7, NIV).

As we grow in our new creation identity, we develop a conscious awareness of the Father's presence with us. This awareness is what allows us to tap into His will and pray powerfully as we co-labor with Christ to express heaven on earth. God's intention is that we walk in a lifestyle of prayer - constantly sensing the intentions of God's realm and releasing His energies wherever we go.

Paul tells the Thessalonians to *"pray without ceasing"* (1 Thessalonians 5:17). This is not an unending stream of meaningless religious pleading. It is a constant release of the realities of heaven into the natural world, empowered by conscious communion with the Creator. Like Paul, our intimate relationship with Jesus allows us to live constantly aware of what the Father is saying and doing. This lifestyle of communication spurns us to pray without ceasing. This constant prayer is what it means to "pray in the Spirit on all occasions."

> "Pray in the Spirit on all occasions with all kinds of prayers and requests. With this in mind, be alert and always keep on praying for all the Lord's people." Ephesians 6:18 (NIV)

Notice the language of constancy in this Ephesians passage: *on all occasions, be alert, always keep on praying*. This verse speaks of a continual human prayer that is saturated with God's presence.

Jude also mentions "praying in the Spirit":

> "But you, dear friends, by building yourselves up in your most holy faith and praying in the Holy Spirit, keep yourselves in God's love as you wait for the mercy of our Lord Jesus Christ to bring you to eternal life." Jude 1:20-21 (NIV)

The prayer "in the Spirit" is quite literally the prayer of God's realm. It is a concentrated communion with heaven and a subsequent "release" of its energies. This aligns with our prophetic mandate to release God's presence wherever we go. As we grow our relationship with God in personal stillness and silence, building up our most holy faith, prayer becomes joyful, life-giving and effortless.

***

This chapter examined Christian worship through the lens of the new creation. As an anointed priesthood, we are called to offer spiritual worship to the living God. This worship is a response to a revelation of God's love for us. Worship that is performed out of duty is not pure worship, but slavish obligation. Worship must be empowered by our love and desire for God, a sentiment echoed beautifully by the Psalmist:

> "Sacrifice and offering you did not desire - but my ears you have opened - burnt offerings and sin offerings you did not require. Then I said, 'Here I am, I have come - it is written about me in the scroll. I desire to do your will, my God; your law is within my heart.'" Psalms 40:6-7 (NIV)

Through the anointing, God has "opened the ears" of His royal priesthood to hear the Good News. Pious religious rituals are no longer necessary because of the once-for-all sacrifice of Jesus Christ. He has poured the Holy Spirit into our hearts, which fuels our desire to know Him in greater and greater measure. Our worship is a stewarding of the presence of Jesus Christ, which has already been given to us through the Holy Spirit.

Worship is the offering of our entire lives in service to God. As we fix our eyes on the image of the Lord Jesus, we are transfigured to become more and more like Him in body, mind, and spirit. As we steward spiritual and physical purity, we progressively receive the kingdom of heaven into our hearts and minds. We are removed from the mental patterning of the world and conformed to the mind of Christ. The kingdom of heaven must be internally realized before it can be externally manifested.

Spiritual worship expresses itself outwardly in many diverse ways. It is not limited to the music we hear on a Sunday morning. Worship is art, poetry, music, theology, sport, and so much more. Anything we do in heartfelt adoration of the Lord is worship that ultimately glorifies Him.

One of the most powerful expressions of our spiritual worship is prayer. Prayer is unceasing communion with the presence of God. All forms of prayer derive from our ability to be in tune with the heart and mind of the Father. Prayer allows us to release God's reality into our situations and circumstances. We are called to unendingly pray in the Spirit of God. The end result is the manifestation of God's reality in our reality, "on earth as it is in heaven."

Chapter Seven

It's All in the Family

There is so much truth in the old saying, "no man is an island." This maxim comes from John Donne's famous seventeenth-century poem. The lesser known second line clarifies the first: "every man is a piece of the continent, a part of the main." The theme of this poem is that no man or woman lives independently of another. We are all part of an interconnected, interdependent whole. We are one global humanity.

This rings especially true for God's anointed royal priesthood. We are a royal people, a holy nation. The plural element is essential here. We are a new spiritual family, an interconnected group of God's beloved sons and daughters. We are all living stones who are being built up to become a new temple for the fullness of God's glorious presence. The material that binds us together is love and the builder is none other than the Holy Spirit.

The Body of Christ is a paradox of sorts. We are many who have become one in Christ. We are a living, breathing representation of unity in diversity. This makes for a very interesting and oftentimes challenging family ethic. Most, if not all, can readily attest that their own family dynamic can be stranger than fiction. How much more so for a global group of people whose distinguishing commonality is an invisible spiritual presence! And yet, family lies at the core of God's plan to rescue the entire universe from the grip of sin and death.

As a kingdom of priests, we do not perform our spiritual duties independent of one other. We need the giftings, graces, and manifestations of the Spirit that others in God's family have to offer. We are a body of interconnected and interdependent moving parts. Love, reverence, and submission to others is how the Body of Christ grows and matures.

God's new creation family is of such importance that half of the epistles seem devoted to behavioral ethics in the Body of Christ. These ethical instructions are less about behaving in a certain way because God or the Bible says to, and more about living worthy of the calling we have received to act as a divinely interconnected family. The essence of our calling as a royal priesthood is to love one another. Jesus Himself testified to this reality when He said, *"A new command I give you: Love one another. As I have loved you, so you must love one another. By this everyone will know that you are my disciples, if you love one another"* (John 13:34-35, NIV). God is love and His kingdom manifests through love. There is one body and one Spirit, who we all partake of. As we drink of the Holy Spirit together, every part of Christ's spiritual body becomes nourished and energized.

> "Live a life worthy of the calling you have received. Be completely humble and gentle; be patient; bearing with one another in love. Make every effort to keep the unity of the Spirit through the bond of peace. There is one body and one Spirit, just as you were called to one hope when you were called; one Lord, one faith, one baptism; one God and Father of all, who is over all and through all and in all." Ephesians 4:1-6 (NIV)

Together, we are a working model of God's new creation humanity. Everyone has a part to play in the Lord's royal family. By understanding our roles in God's new family, we awaken to the fullness of His plan and intention for the Body of Christ.

Father Abraham Had Many Sons

The gospel is ultimately about the restoration and reunification of God's children. Our commonality is a lavish experience of God's Holy Spirit. God's children have been "born again" into a new kind of existence that is characterized and empowered by His presence. We bond together when we fix our eyes on this unseen reality. We run into problems when we lose our sense of unity and singularity of purpose.

Spiritual family is a core component of the new creation that is woefully under-emphasized in the modern American church. We like our gospel packed up like a school lunch- quick to eat, easy to digest, with no mess. We live in a digital age of sound bytes and Instagram likes. This makes it easy for us to suppress or ignore our call to live in intimate community with each other.

There is an easy-to-miss verse nestled in the middle of Galatians that has the power to dramatically shift our understanding of family in relation to the gospel:

> "Scripture foresaw that God would justify the Gentiles by faith, and announced the gospel in advance to Abraham: 'All nations will be blessed through you.' So those who rely on faith are blessed along with Abraham, the man of faith."
> Galatians 3:7-8 (NIV)

What does it mean here that God announced the gospel in advance to Abraham? These verses make no mention of heaven, hell, or the salvation of the human soul! What does it mean to "rely on faith" in order to be "blessed along with Abraham?" What does this have to do with the gospel?

We need some quick context. The book of Galatians was written to address the religionism that had seeped into the first-century church. Jewish believers in the Jesus movement were demanding that non-Jews become circumcised in order to be included in God's new creation family. This was flagrant error, as God's new humanity is not defined by special religious observances or physical characteristics, but by the presence of the Holy Spirit. The Holy Spirit allows all equal access to God.

The gospel is related to Abraham because he is the father of the Judeo-Christian faith. Initially, Abraham was a "nobody," just a random joe-schmo who lived in Mesopotamia thousands of years before the incarnation of Christ. God appeared to this man Abraham and promised him that he would be lavishly blessed as the father of many nations. The scriptures tell us that Abraham responded by trusting God, and God in turn "credited" this trust as righteousness (right-standing):

> "So also Abraham 'believed God, and it was credited to him as righteousness.' Understand, then that those who have faith are children of Abraham." Galatians 3:6-7 (NIV)

The main point is that we are all Abraham's "children" through the Holy Spirit. Abraham is indeed the father of many nations because his faith is now our faith! Like Abraham before us, when we believe God, He brings us into right-standing (righteousness) with Himself. This gives us access to the promise of God's prosperity and spiritual blessings. The Body of Christ is now one global family that is defined by the Holy Spirit, simple trust in the living God, and His lavish promises to Abraham.

The "gospel," therefore, is less about our post-earth destiny and more about the restoration and unity of mankind. God's "good news" is that the Holy Spirit has restored humanity's access to heaven (God's reality) and allows us to pursue this reality in empowered fellowship with one another. Not only this, but God has given all of His sons and daughters access to the covenant blessings of Abraham and his descendants. What matters now is not political, racial, physical, religious, and social divisions, but the role of the "Israel of God" in the new creation:

> "May I never boast except in the cross of our Lord Jesus Christ, through whom the world (the old creation order) has been crucified to me, and I to the world. Neither circumcision (outward, physical religious acts) nor uncircumcision means anything; what counts is the new creation (denoted by the renewing presence of the Holy Spirit). Peace and mercy to all who follow this rule and to the Israel of God (the new creation humanity)." Galatians 6:14-16 (NIV), parenthetical annotations mine

> "So in Jesus Christ you are all children of God through faith, for all of you who were baptized into Christ have clothed yourselves with Christ. There is neither Jew nor Gentile, neither slave nor free, nor is there male and female, for you are all one in Christ Jesus. If you belong to Christ, then you are Abraham's seed, and heirs according to the promise." Galatians 3:26-29 (NIV)

God's children do not retain the thinking patterns of the old creation order that is in the process of passing away. The Holy Spirit empowers us to think and act like Christ as individuals and communities. As we do, the kingdom of heaven is made manifest. The sons of God do not behave like Christ because they have to, but because they love to. The new creation reality empowers us to think and behave differently. God trusts us with the responsibility of stewarding the divine presence that is in us and others. The new humanity is responsible for shining the true light of Christ into a dark and unbelieving world. How can we manifest the kingdom if worldly thinking patterns and sinful divisions remain in our midst?

We must view no one "according to the flesh," according to the old creation order's way of thinking. We must consider ourselves and others as children of God who are working together in unity to achieve God's purposes on Planet Earth. We are the children of Abraham, a family of faith that spans the globe and shares in God's lavish blessings. This reality must dominate our thinking. New creation humans think *globally*.

> "Here there is no Gentile or Jew, circumcised or uncircumcised, barbarian, Scythian, slave or free, but Christ is all, and is in all. Therefore, as God's chosen people, holy and dearly loved, clothe yourselves with compassion, kindness, humility, gentleness and patience. Bear with each other and forgive one another if any of you have a grievance against someone. Forgive as the Lord forgave you. And over all these virtues put on love, which binds them all together in perfect unity." Colossians 3:11-14 (NIV)

Bread and Wine

For many today, the centerpiece of the family experience is a shared meal at suppertime. This is when we come together daily to share stories, laugh, cry, argue and, most importantly, eat. There is a strange sacredness to the family dinner. Something profound happens in the unseen when we come together to share a meal. Abraham's sons have their own special kind of "family dinner." It is called the Lord's Table, or communion.

The Lord's Table is where we come together as a united family to remind ourselves of the spiritual feast we have in Jesus Christ. The Psalmist writes that God prepares a table for us in the presence of our enemies (Psalm 23:5). He satisfies the thirsty and fills the hungry with good things (Psalm 107:9). As God's children, we continually feast on His spiritual blessings and covenant promises. Spiritual food is the richest of foods. As the Holy Spirit says: *"On this mountain the Lord Almighty will prepare a feast of rich food for all peoples, a banquet of aged wine - the best of meats and the finest of wines"* (Isaiah 25:6, NIV). The Lord's Table binds us together as one family in the kingdom promises of God.

Communion is so much more than a morose reminder that Jesus died for our sins. Many of us today never move beyond understanding that the bread represents the broken body of Jesus and the wine represents His spilled blood. Communion is therefore only a contemplative experience of Christ's suffering on the cross. There is so much more to the Lord's Table than this! Communion is powerful and has cosmic implications for God's covenant people. To understand communion at a deeper level is to more fully grasp our identity as Christ's new creation family.

It is no mystery that the Lord Himself gave to the Church the ritual of communion:

> "While they were eating, Jesus took bread, and when he had given thanks, he broke it and gave it to his disciples, saying: 'Take and eat; this is my body.' Then he took a cup, and when he had given thanks, he gave it to them, saying, 'Drink from it, all of you. This is my blood of the new covenant,

which is poured out for many for the forgiveness of sins.'"
Matthew 26:26-28 (NIV)

"The Lord Jesus, on the night he was betrayed, took bread, and when he had given thanks, he broke it and said, 'This is my body, which is for you; do this in remembrance of me.' In the same way, after supper he took the cup, saying, 'This cup is the new covenant in my blood; do this, whenever you drink it, in remembrance of me.' For whenever you eat this bread and drink this cup, you proclaim the Lord's death until he comes." 1 Corinthians 11:23-26 (NIV)

When Christ said, "do this in remembrance of me," I don't think He thought that any of the disciples would actually forget about him. This "remembrance" is more of a meditation on the *total work* of Christ: the reconciliation of humanity to the living God. It is to bring to mind our responsibility to steward the kingdom of God within the Body of Christ until its fullest consummation. The meditation of communion involves two essential elements: the bread and the wine. I would like to highlight the relevance of these two elements in our understanding of the new creation.

To partake of the bread is to partake of the body of Christ. There are implications here. First, communion traditionally features one single loaf of bread that is divided into pieces for each individual. The individual pieces are part of a greater unified whole. This obviously symbolizes our unity in diversity. Together, we partake of the one risen Christ, who is Jesus. But what exactly does it mean to "eat" His body?

Jesus Christ is the divine nature and human nature working together synergistically in one person. The scriptures tell us that Christ is now *"over all and through all and in all"* and that He has *"ascended higher than all the heavens, in order to fill the whole universe"* (Ephesians 4:6-10, NIV). Paul says, *"He is before all things, and in him all things hold together"* (Colossians 1:17, NIV). It is hard to comprehend with mere human reasoning but the glorified Christ, who is a man, now fills the entire universe with His presence. Through the Holy Spirit, we have been united with Him in this regard. God has raised us up with

Christ and seated us with him in the heavenly realms.[46] This is why Paul can write that the Church is *"His body, the fullness of Him who fills everything in every way"* (Ephesians 1:22, NIV). Therefore, to eat the bread together as one family is to meditate on the reality that we are the fullness of Christ on Planet Earth and beyond. We embody His presence and will continue to do so when we leave our earthly existence and move into the heavenly realms.

The bread of communion is the glorious reminder that we, as one global spiritual family, sit with the ascended Lord in the spiritual realm. The king of the universe has invited us to participate in His great cosmic reign over all things seen and unseen. The bread also reminds us that He holds the entire universe together and actively energizes it with His presence. Everything that exists is from Him and for Him.

The wine of communion is the blood of Christ. We know that the blood of Christ has covered humanity, effectively freeing us from the shackles of sin and darkness.

> "In him we have redemption (renewal) through his blood, the forgiveness of sins, in accordance with the riches of God's grace (energizing presence) that he lavished on us."
> Ephesians 1:7 (NIV), parenthetical annotations mine

Forgiveness of sins is not the be-all-end-all for Christians. It is only a beginning, an open door that allows us into the reality of the new creation and the lavish spiritual blessings of God. Paul confirms this in the verse that immediately follows the one above:

> "With all wisdom and understanding, he made known to us the mystery of his will according to his good pleasure, which he purposed in Christ, to be put into effect when the times reach their fulfillment - **to bring unity to all things in heaven and on earth**." Ephesians 1:8 (NIV)

---

[46] "And God raised us up with Christ and seated us with him in in the heavenly realms in Christ Jesus, in order that in the coming ages he might show the incomparable riches of his grace, expressed in his kindness to us in Christ Jesus." Ephesians 2:6-7 (NIV)

Paul writes that the ultimate purpose of Christ's blood is to bring total reconciliation between the things of heaven and the things of earth. This is the essence of the new creation. The blood and the sacrifice of Christ are the open door to this reality. Having been restored to God through Christ, we are the means by which God is putting this cosmic plan for unity between the seen and unseen into motion:

> "Once you were alienated from God and were enemies in your minds because of your evil behavior. But now he has reconciled you by Christ's physical body through death to present you holy in his sight, without blemish and free from accusation...For God was pleased to have all his fullness dwell in him, and through him to reconcile all things, whether things on earth or things in heaven, by making peace through his blood, shed on the cross." Colossians 1:21-22, 19-20 (NIV)

It is wonderful and honorable to remember the sufferings of Christ on the cross through the wine of communion. But we would do well to remember that His suffering also purchased something for us - the fullness of the kingdom! When we drink the wine together as one family, we are reminded of our shared mission to bring unity between the things of heaven and the things of earth. This happens as we partner with each other and God to advance His kingdom.

It is worth mentioning that the Hebrews (and therefore the Bible writers) considered blood to be the very life force of created beings. When Christ poured out His blood for us, He offered to us the totality of His divine life. To drink of Christ's blood then is to participate in His life. This is His eternal life which is actively given to us by the Holy Spirit. Because we are united with Christ, His presence empowers us to live in holiness, purity, and heavenly productivity.

There is another glorious subtlety hidden in the wine of communion. Blood brings to mind family and lineage. As the Body of Christ, we share the blood of Christ. We are a new humanity, a new class of human beings who carry eternal life and embody the realities of the new creation. Peter writes that we have been *"born again, not of perishable seed, but of imperishable, through the living and enduring word of God"* (1 Peter 1:23, NIV). We are "born again" in the sense that we have received the Holy Spirit, who fills us with the eternal life of Christ. We are like a bride who has consummated her marriage to her husband. The result is an entirely new kind of life that fills us and grows within us.

We now steward the divine bloodline as a global family. Before Christ, humanity collectively carried and compounded the sin of Adam, which resulted in death upon death. But now, in Christ, sin's devastation upon mankind has objectively come to an end. Having been freed from its shackles, the Body of Christ is a new humanity that stewards God's eternal life. As we nurture this new life that is already within us, we will experience its fruit in greater and greater measure.

It will take many generations for the fullness of this life to be realized in and through the Body of Christ. This is a hard truth that requires patience and vision on our end. We must adopt a cosmic perspective that looks beyond our current time in history to glimpse the fullness of what God has planned for the human race. We are responsible for stewarding the kingdom and making inroads into its fullness. This is why the Holy Spirit says the following in Isaiah:

> "A voice of one calling in the wilderness: 'Prepare the way for the Lord; make straight in the desert a highway for our God. Every valley shall be raised up, every mountain and hill made low; the rough ground shall become level, the rugged places a plain. And the glory of the Lord will be revealed, and all people will see it together." Isaiah 40:3-5 (NIV)

> "And it will be said: 'Build up, build up, prepare the road! Remove the obstacles out of the way of my people.'" Isaiah 57:14 (NIV)

> "Pass through, pass through the gates! Prepare the way for the people! Build up, build up the highway! Remove the stones. Raise a banner for the nations." Isaiah 62:10 (NIV)

The Body of Christ removes "obstacles" by demolishing arguments and vain pretensions that exalt themselves against Christ and His kingdom.[47] We build a "road" and a "highway" by walking on divine understandings established by Christ and His apostles (past and present). But, most importantly, we become fruitful and multiply in the eternal life of God. The results are good works and godly offspring who carry the inheritance of the kingdom, steward it and, in turn, pass it on to their children. This is why the scriptures say, *"Has not the one God made you? You belong to him in body and spirit. And what does the one God seek? Godly offspring"* (Malachi 2:15, NIV).

The wine of communion, therefore, is a reminder that we together steward the blood of Christ and the realities of the kingdom of heaven. Having been born again of "imperishable seed," we steward the divine bloodline by the presence of the Holy Spirit. There is an inheritance in the Spirit that we and our descendants are responsible for seeking, nurturing and bringing into realization.

This understanding of the bread and the wine of the Lord's Table breathes new life into a centuries-old religious ritual. The bread and the wine speak of a timeless cosmic family and this special family's role in the new creation. With this being said, we must not approach communion lightly. Communion is serious business because it sums up the new creation in two physical elements. It is the very heart of God in symbolic form. Because of this, Paul writes the following:

> "Whoever eats the bread or drinks the cup of the Lord in an unworthy manner will be guilty of sinning against the body and blood of the Lord. Everyone ought to examine themselves before they eat of the bread and drink from the cup. For those who eat and drink without discerning the body of Christ eat and drink judgment on themselves. That is why so many among you are weak and sick, and a number of you have fallen asleep...So then, my brothers and sisters,

---

[47] "We demolish arguments and every pretension that sets itself up against the knowledge of God, and we take captive every thought to make it obedient to Christ." 2 Corinthians 10:5 (NIV)

when you gather to eat, you should all eat together." 1 Corinthians 11:27-33 (NIV)

This is an often-misunderstood passage from 1 Corinthians. To take communion in an "unworthy manner" does not mean to participate even though we may feel damned and separated from God because of some hidden sin. Paul makes it clear the offense to God comes when we fail to "discern the Body of Christ." This means that we fail to regard our brothers and sisters in Christ with love and inclusiveness. Paul wrote this letter because believers in Corinth were not of one mind and heart when they came together at the Lord's Table. This violation of divine love had its natural consequences, as is made clear by the Corinthians becoming weak and sick.

The focal point of communion is Christ's victory over sin and death in order to create a new humanity. We should approach the bread and wine with a deep reverence for Christ and an honor and respect for each other. The two elements, the bread and the wine, are symbols of the new creation in miniature form. As one global family, we sit at the Lord's Table and partake together of His limitless kingdom blessings.

The Dust of the Earth

The priests of the Old Covenant performed their duties to God in the physical temple or tabernacle. As New Covenant priests, we minister to God through the Body of Christ, which is a new spiritual temple and the earthly location of God's manifest presence. Jesus said, *"Anyone who has seen me has seen the Father"* (John 14:9, NIV). The Body of Christ is filled with the divine presence of the Father because of Christ's presence within us. God the Father is now *"over all and through all and in all"* (Ephesians 4:6, NIV). An essential role of New Covenant priests is to minister to each other with acts of loving service. Acts of love toward others are the building blocks of the kingdom of heaven. They reveal the heart and glory of the Father.

The parable of the sheep and the goats in Matthew 25 is an illustration of this truth. The parable speaks of judgment, when the Son of Man "comes in glory" and gathers the nations to Him. The king arrives and begins separating the sheep from the goats. To the sheep He says, *"Come, you who are blessed by my Father; take your inheritance, the kingdom prepared for you since the creation of the* world. *For I was hungry and you gave me something to eat, I was thirsty and you gave me something to drink, I was a stranger and you invited me in, I needed clothes and you clothed me, I was sick and you looked after me, I was in prison and you came to visit me...Whatever you did for one of the least of these brothers and sisters, you did for me."* He rewards the sheep with eternal life and a place in the kingdom. He sends the goats (those who did not manifest loving actions) into punishment.[48]

This parable speaks to a *current* reality. God is already in the process of separating the "sheep" from the "goats." The Lord's main point here is that intellectual faith means absolutely nothing in the kingdom of God if it does not result in loving acts of service. The kingdom of heaven requires both internal realization and external manifestation. Knowledge puffs up, but tangible Christ-like acts make God's reality our reality.

We are called to bring this ethic to humanity at large. Our "practice field" is the Body of Christ, our brothers and sisters in the faith who share the Holy Spirit. It is ridiculous to think we can love those outside the Body of Christ without developing genuine, Christ-like love for those within it. Our spiritual family is where we can effectively practice acts of love and learn how we as individuals fit into God's greater global picture. If we can do it in the Church, it will happen effortlessly outside of it.

The Body is a vast, interconnected system of moving parts who must rely on each other to grow and mature. We are called to live productive lives for the kingdom. Productivity implies a goal and the means to obtain this goal. For us, the goal is the fullness of the kingdom of heaven. The means by which we reach this fullness are the manifestations, giftings and graces of the Holy Spirit. The key to understand is that we have all been given a grace by the Lord to put into practice. This "grace" is not just mercy and forgiveness, but an energizing supply of God's presence that allows us to live holy and productive lives for the sake of the kingdom. Concerning these graces in the Body, Paul writes the following:

> "Now about the [graces] of the Spirit, brothers and sisters,
> I do not want you to be uninformed...There are different
> kinds of [graces], but the same Spirit distributes them.

---

[48] See Matthew 25:31-46 for the full parable.

> There are different kinds of service, but the same Lord. There are different kinds of working, but in all of them and in everyone it is the same God at work. Now to each one the manifestation of the Spirit is given for the common good." 1 Corinthians 12:1-7 (NIV)

Paul goes on to arbitrarily mention some of these graces of the Holy Spirit, which include not only Spirit-empowered "giftings" (tongues, miracles, prophecy, wisdom, etc.) but also "offices" such as apostle, prophet, and teacher. The million-dollar takeaway here is that Paul is *not trying to establish a theology or exclusive list of spiritual "giftings."* He is mentioning some of the ways Christ may choose to express Himself through individuals in the Body at any given point in time. A "manifestation" of the Holy Spirit is some sort of tangible expression of the risen Christ that ultimately serves to build up the kingdom. The manifestation may be a singular event such as a prophecy or healing, or it may be a particular calling on an individual for a season or a lifetime.

With manifestations, giftings, and graces, we would do well to keep in mind the words of Paul: *what do you have that you did not receive?* (1 Corinthians 4:7). As anointed priests, we are in union with the ascended Christ. We died with Him on the cross. We no longer live, but He lives within us. As we yield to Him, He will do what He wants to do through us.

Our thinking in this particular area of spirituality is far too immature. We love to claim gifts and titles as endowments, as if they have been deposited into some sort of personal spiritual account by the Lord. This is why we have individuals running around saying things like, "I have the gift of tongues and prophecy" or "my name is Prophet Michael," as if these gifts belonged to us exclusively.

I am adamant about this because there are many who would prefer to define themselves by a particular gifting or calling rather than the presence of the ascended Christ. We can become so focused on growing one particular gifting or calling that we lose focus of the central element: Christ's presence. Our entire worldview can become defined by the "gift" that we feel God has given us. This can blind us, leave us susceptible to pride, and prevent us from operating in a well-rounded spirituality. Spiritual "specialists" in the Body of

New Creation Spirituality: Christianity in the 21st Century and Beyond

Christ must be careful not to leave the rest of the group behind in order to focus on themselves. Without regard for the Body at large, they will lose connection to the head, who is Christ.

We are all unique individuals who share the same Christ and form one global body. This Christ has blessed us in the heavenly realms with every spiritual blessing.[49] These blessings are not limited to what is considered miraculous or extraordinary. Acts of service are just as valuable to Christ as miracles are. Everything should be done in the name of love for the building of the kingdom. Christ and the apostles make clear love is the greatest spiritual manifestation in the kingdom of God.

The Christ in me sees and honors the Christ in you. This expression should characterize our desire to build up others inside and outside the Body. It is less about striving to figure out how our autonomous giftings can possibly work together in harmony, and more about recognizing and honoring what Christ is doing in and through others at any given moment. When we recognize what Christ is doing in others and seek to honor it with our actions, the Father is pleased.

Our function in the Body is entirely dependent on the will of the Father. This is why He is called the potter and we are called the clay.[50] Clay can be reheated and reshaped to fit the desire of the craftsman. Our individual function in the Body of Christ is in constant evolution. To fit ourselves into a fixed understanding of who we feel we are limits our spiritual growth and potential.

God promised to Abraham that his descendants would be like the "dust of the earth."[51] Dust is unsettled and easily picked up to be carried by the wind. We are God's dust and the wind is His Holy Spirit. We must allow ourselves to be picked up and carried by the will of the Father. This is why the Lord said, *"Foxed have dens and birds have nests, but the Son of Man has no place to lay his*

---

[49] "Praise be to the God and Father of our Lord Jesus Christ, who has blessed us in the heavenly realms with every spiritual blessing in Christ." Ephesians 1:3 (NIV)

[50] "Yet you, Lord, are our Father. We are the clay, you are the potter; we are all the work of your hand." Isaiah 64:8 (NIV)

[51] "I will make your offspring like the dust of the earth, so that if anyone could count the dust, then your offspring could be counted." Genesis 13:16 (NIV)

head" (Matthew 8:20, NIV). The Lord was completely yielded to the spontaneous will of the Father. This is our model and pattern, especially in the area of servitude to the corporate body of believers. The prayer of our heart should match that of the Lord's mother, Mary: "*I am the Lord's servant, let it be done to me according to thy will*" (Luke 1:38).

***

God's anointed priesthood is called to do life in fellowship. Fellowship is family. We are all God's sons and daughters who constitute a new global spiritual family. The distinguishing factor of our family bond is the presence of the Holy Spirit. Those led by the Spirit of God are the sons and daughters of God. In union with God and unity with each other, we are called to steward and advance the realities of God's kingdom.

God has given this new spiritual family lavish giftings which allow us to bless each other and the nations of the world. These gifts are enabled by the presence of the Holy Spirit, who gives us full access to Christ's riches in glory. In the light of this glory, all external considerations that may have once separated and divided us disappear.

Communion is a glorious reminder that we sit at the Lord's Table as one global family, united in love. The bread reminds us that we are one body of believers who share a common Lord. This Lord has ascended into heaven in order to fill the entire universe. Having been brought into His fullness, He invites us to do the same. The wine reminds us that His spilled blood has forgiven all of our sins. This blood now courses through our veins. We steward the royal bloodline, the spiritual lineage of the King. We are a new humanity called to rule and reign alongside Christ.

As an interconnected, interdependent family, we serve one another and humanity at large by manifesting the Holy Spirit. The manifestation of the Holy Spirit is loving acts of service that range in scope from the "mundane" to the "miraculous." As we yield ourselves to the perfect will of the Father, He uses us as He pleases to build the kingdom of God. As we learn to love our spiritual family and grow in acts of service, the Body of Christ matures, and the reality of the new creation becomes manifest in greater and greater measure.

Chapter Eight

The Good News Couriers

A few years ago, I was vacationing with family in an area that featured a bustling, expansive boardwalk, complete with roller coasters, a waterpark, and countless other attractions. One evening, during a walk alone on the boardwalk, I noticed a large group of young people handing out flyers. I had a hunch they were Christians, so I made my way over and struck up a conversation with a young man (let's call him Jason). Jason kindly informed me that they were a Christian group who had rented out the boardwalk's chapel to do evangelistic work. I had found my people! I excitedly told Jason that I would be eager to join them later that evening for their first service. At this point in my spiritual journey, I had been flowing in spiritual graces such as healing and prophecy for years. I imagined radical healings breaking out on the boardwalk and dozens of people coming to know Christ. The boardwalk would be changed forever!

I returned to the chapel a few hours later and found a seat close to the front row. Some people from the organization were still handing out flyers to passersby. They had been doing so for hours so I figured there would soon be some sort of crowd. People were going to hear the gospel! I was especially excited because this group seemed so young and energetic. I was slightly nervous but also thrilled to take a public stand for Christ in solidarity with these brave believers.

Soon, the presentation began. The lights dimmed and microphone feedback burst uncomfortably through the portable speaker system. *No problem*, I thought. Another young man (let's call him Stu) began a prayer to open the meeting.

"Dear Father God," Stu began, "we humbly approach your throne and ask that you would shine your light upon this dark generation. You know that this boardwalk is evil and that everything it stands for is just as evil. We know that we are depraved sinners and that we are in desperate need of your grace. Please come and touch peoples' lives. Amen."

Okay, I thought, *familiar religionist language and not exactly the full truth of the gospel, but God can work through it*! I glimpsed over my shoulder and noticed that I was one of three people in the entire chapel. Near the front entrance, crowds rushed past. No one seemed to give a hoot about what was going on. I gulped and slinked down deeper into my seat. Hadn't they been passing out flyers for hours? *I am not ashamed of the gospel of Christ, I am not ashamed of the gospel of Christ*, I began to repeat to myself.

It pains me to say it, but what happened next was downright excruciating. I respect the boldness of my brothers and sisters in Christ, but I honestly think that what transpired on stage did more harm than good. It was a "Christian" skit - one of the corny ones that you would be probably familiar with if you had any sort of involvement with a youth group in the 90s. It involved a group of saints, sinners, a sacrificed lamb of God (played by a young woman in a costume), and, of course, a fiery depiction of an unbeliever burning in Hell. Boos and jeers from the passing crowds were unexpected additions to the already uncomfortable drama unfolding on stage. Finally, after what seemed like an eternity (no pun intended), an altar call was given. Being the only one left at that point (the other two visitors had long since disappeared), I quietly snuck away and disappeared into the crowd.

A few days later, I passed by the chapel again. The group was still there and planning for evening activities. I honestly felt bad for Jason because I knew He loved Jesus and we had connected well during our brief conversation a few days earlier. I asked him how the week was going for the group. "It's fine," he said, rather sheepishly.

I wanted to encourage him, so I pried a little bit more. "What's going on? How have things been this week?"

"It's tough," he replied. "Not many people seem very interested in the gospel here. It's easier in the Midwest where we are from."

I nodded. "Any conversions?" I asked.

"Maybe one or two," Jason replied distractedly. This was clearly not the same Jason I had talked to several nights before. He was exhausted, his excitement now replaced with an apparent apathy.

"Hey man, I just really want to encourage you. You're taking bold steps for Jesus. It is really evident you are an amazing person and an incredible leader." With this, his face lit up. I invited him to pray for me, which he did. I said a few more words to encourage him and bid him farewell.

I share this story because it is directly related to the next duty of God's anointed priesthood: evangelism. To evangelize is to spread the Word of Christ to the people. Gospel literally means "good news." As God's anointed priests, we are called to spread the good news about Christ throughout the globe. We proclaim a radical, life-changing message. If it isn't good news, it isn't the gospel.

What bothered me so much about my experience on the boardwalk was that a message was presented to the unbelieving public as the "gospel," when, in reality, it was an affront to the finished work of the cross. As I have made clear throughout this book, the gospel is not just about sin, heaven, and hell. The "good news" isn't that we aren't going to hell. Forgiveness of sin is not the crux of the gospel - restored relationship with God is. The forgiveness of sin only opens the door to the reality of the new creation. The gospel is this: through the forgiveness of sins and the giving of the Holy Spirit, Jesus Christ has united humanity to God forever, initiating an entirely new creation.

Religionists focus on the depravity of man, a life-long (losing) battle with sin, and archaic, ineffective theological teachings and traditions. The religionist gospel revolves around these core elements, not a living Presence that pervades our reality and invites us to participate in His. Religionist

Christianity is an intellectual institution with theoretical tenants that must be assented to in order to be "saved." Faith is about attending church to hear more intellectual ideas about the Bible so that behavior can be modified to match "proper" theological teaching. This is spiritual slavery disguised as a relationship with God. This "gospel" should be avoided at all costs.

What I witnessed that night was an overdramatic presentation of the Protestant/evangelical understanding of the gospel. Five centuries ago, in an era with very different spiritual and social attitudes, this type of gospel presentation may have been very effective. The reason for this is that the revelation of the Protestant Reformation was, at that time, freshly anointed and, therefore, powerful and effective. Born in a particular cultural and religious context, it met the spiritual challenges of its time beautifully. This understanding and approach to the gospel will soon fade and disappear because it is no longer effective in meeting the spiritual needs of the current era. If it has any effectiveness left, it is purely because of God's grace.

This book is about a radical rediscovery of Christ's gospel. His gospel has everything to do with union with God and a lavish experience of His presence. Our evangelism, our spreading of the good news, must therefore revolve around this reality. God has not left us without amazing models, particularly Jesus Christ, the master evangelist Himself. We can look to His life for profound insights on how to evangelize in the new creation.

The Master Evangelist

The gospels of Matthew, Mark, Luke, and John paint a remarkably clear picture of new creation evangelism. Peter succinctly summarizes this evangelistic approach beautifully during a speech that is documented in the book of Acts: *"God anointed Jesus of Nazareth with the Holy Spirit and power, and he went around doing good and healing all who were under the power of the devil, because God was with Him"* (Acts 10:38, NIV).

Jesus Christ flowed in the Holy Spirit, doing what He saw the Father doing and saying what He heard the Father saying. The gospels are complete with examples of Jesus ushering in the kingdom of God through healings, miracles, spiritual teachings, and acts of love. He gave special attention to the poor, disenfranchised, and downtrodden, but did not neglect any who desired the kingdom. His teachings were not about adhering to a religious system in order to appease the anger of God. Jesus inaugurated a new reality in the earthly realm - God's reality. *"Change your perspective!"* Jesus preached. *"For the kingdom of heaven has come to earth!"* (Matthew 4:17). Jesus embodied the reality of the new creation. It is not something that we objectively need to wait for. It has been accomplished through His death and resurrection. What remains is our subjective experience of Jesus' victory on the cross.

The way Jesus lived in the gospels exemplifies new creation spirituality and evangelism. A light has dawned on humanity. Jesus is that light and we now shine with Him.[52] We share the light of Christ and are called to be torchbearers who illuminate and embody the realities of the new creation. Jesus says in Matthew 5:14-16, *"You are the light of the world. A town built on a hill cannot be hidden...let your light shine before others, that they may see your good deeds and glorify your Father in heaven."* As the new temple of the living God, we are the "town" Jesus is referring to. The "hill" is Golgotha, where Jesus was crucified. The new creation humanity stands in victory upon this hill of death. *Where, O death, is your victory. Where, O death, is your sting?* Death's victory was swallowed up and destroyed on the cross.

We could rake through the gospels and I could give many practical examples of how to approach evangelism in the same manner of Jesus, but that is not my goal. Rather, I want to encourage us to view Jesus as the model and pattern for new creation evangelism. Christ boldly and unabashedly shared a new reality paradigm with people from all walks of life. In love, He invited others to join Him in an experience of the Father's kingdom. This kingdom is characterized by freedom, healing, joy, peace, and an intimate relationship with the heavenly Father through the Holy Spirit. Jesus didn't proselytize in order to win converts.

"For God so loved the world, that He gave His only begotten son, that whoever believes in Him shall not perish, but have eternal life," says John 3:16. We often forget the next verse: *"For God did not send his Son to condemn the world, but to save the world through him."* Christ did not come in the flesh to *condemn* the world, but to *redeem* and *restore* it. Our actions on His behalf are motivated by this truth. We are

---

[52] "When Jesus spoke again to the people, he said, 'I am the light of the world. Whoever follows me will never walk in darkness, but will have the light of life." John 8:6 (NIV)

ministers of restoration and reconciliation, not portents of wrath and destruction. We embody a new reality that God invites everyone to be a part of. It is no longer about *what* we know, but *who* we know. Great evangelism is not about getting as many people "saved" as possible. It is about loving God and loving our neighbor. There will be glorious fruit if we simply rest in this reality.

As Christian evangelists, we need to sit down and honestly reflect on our motivation. Is it a genuine love for people and a vision for the new creation, or a thirst to spread a religious ideology? Is our desire to preach Christ based on insecurity and a deep need for religious validation, or a genuine conviction that we are radically loved by our Father in heaven? Do we act because we *love* to, or because we feel like we *need* to? Do we really care about people or do we want to appear spiritual in the minds of others? Do we want people healed, empowered, and autonomous, or do we want them dependent on the pattern of teaching that we follow?

Above all, we must put on the mind of Christ. We must be sensitive to what the Father is saying and doing at any given moment. We must view life through the eyes of divine love. If our motivation isn't love or the prompting of the Father, our actions are empty religious activity that mean nothing to God.

We so often forget that Jesus' primary opponents were not the common people, but the entrenched religious institution. The crowds flocked to the powerful spiritual atmosphere present in and through Christ. The religious leaders hated Jesus because He embodied a freedom, wholeness, and divinity independent from the established religious system. He was a threat to their power over the minds and hearts of the common people. He offended their love for money, influence, and control. Most of all, He violated their religious pride and the trust they placed in their human knowledge about God. This is why they plotted to have Him killed.

This may be an unpopular opinion, but I believe if our evangelism isn't attractive to people, it isn't the gospel. This doesn't mean we "water down" the gospel. We don't need to. The gospel is about the power of God that brings salvation.[53] An intellectual faith saves no one. The message saves no one. Standing on a street corner or going door to door telling people Jesus loves them won't do much in the long run. A tangible experience of God's power will. People are drawn to the real gospel because it connects with our very DNA. We are created to live in intimate relationship with our Creator and to experience His power and goodness. Faith restores humanity to this state and allows us to partake of God's reality. Eternal life is attractive because it is latent in our destiny.

I have had more evangelistic "success" in the last three years than I have had in over twenty years of being a Christian. I used to worry I wasn't doing enough for God. Deep down, I always felt that I needed to do more in order to make God happy and somehow prove my faith. Pastors and ministers used to intimidate me. When I began to understand my identity in the new creation, my fears began to dissolve. God began to gradually fill my life with opportunities to share His love and power. I didn't need to do anything. I just rested in my relationship with Him and let Him do what He wanted to do. I realized I could make just as much of a difference for the kingdom as a missionary in Africa. Evangelism is easy. If you're trying hard to save souls, you're doing it wrong.

Above all, the gospel is about a radically restructured lifestyle paradigm. Jesus demonstrated this lifestyle during His ministry on earth and continues to empower us to do the same. It is about a new state of *being*, a new way of life that is characterized by God's empowering presence. As we grow in this new way of being, God's power flows through us effortlessly to impact our environments with His love.

Tongues of Fire

One of my favorite moments in the entire Bible is the day of Pentecost, described in the book of Acts. On Pentecost, the disciples are in quarantine, waiting for the ascended Christ to "send the Holy Spirit." What would soon take place would change their lives forever. The scriptures put it like this:

---

[53] "For I am not ashamed of the gospel, because it is the power of God that brings salvation to everyone who believes: first to the Jew, then to the Gentile." Romans 1:16 (NIV)

> "When the day of Pentecost came, they were all together in one place. Suddenly a sound like the blowing of a violent wind came from heaven and filled the whole house where they were sitting. They saw what seemed to be tongues of fire that separated and came to rest on each of them. All of them were filled with the Holy Spirit and began to speak in other tongues as the Spirit enabled them." Acts 2:1-4 (NIV)

The disciples then poured out into the streets of Jerusalem and began evangelizing. Many "God-fearing Jews from every nation under heaven" were amazed that they were hearing divine truths being spontaneously spoken by men and women who did not speak their language. The scriptures say that about three thousand became believers of Christ on that day.[54] This is a very well-known passage of Scripture, but if we dive a little deeper in our understanding, we can learn a wonderful lesson and apply it to our topic of new creation evangelism.

This event from Acts is obviously literal - it really happened. But, true to form, Luke (the author of Acts) colors the narrative with symbolism, metaphor and allusion. Fire is a powerful symbol of purification. "Tongues of fire" appear in Isaiah as a metaphor for divine judgment that will consume idolatry and iniquity.[55] This allusion would certainly not be missed by a first-century Jew hearing or reading Luke's narrative in Acts. So, what is the spiritual meaning of the tongues of fire that came to rest on the disciples?

The tongues of fire are a metaphor for the purifying message of divine love. As the cross reveals to us, love is the judgment. The tongues of fire are a testimony to God's judgment on sin and death. God's love is a consuming fire that burns up anything that stands between us and Him. Acts tells us that those in Jerusalem were amazed that they heard the disciples declaring the wonders of God in their own tongues. The foreign peoples were encountering

---

[54] "Those who accepted his message were baptized, and about three thousand were added to their number that day." Acts 2:41 (NIV)

[55] "Therefore, as tongues of fire lick up straw and as dry grass sinks down in the flames, so their roots will decay and their flowers blow away like dust; for they have rejected the law of the Lord Almighty and spurned the word of the Holy One of Israel." Isaiah 5:24 (NIV)

a powerful, tangible demonstration of God's love, manifesting itself through the disciples in the form of other languages.

The spiritual implications of Pentecost should blaze before our eyes. Are our tongues alit with the fire of heaven or the fire of hell?[56] Is our message one of love that meets others right where they are in order to declare the wonderful works of God? Pentecost wasn't just about God winning over foreigners through a powerful manifestation of His Spirit. It was about connecting the lost to the powerful message of divine love.

On Pentecost, the non-believing Jews were met powerfully by God in a way that was powerful, impactful, and relevant. He spoke to them about His wonders in their own language, something that they could understand. The disciples and apostles weren't trying to win anyone over to an ideology. They were testifying to a reality that was making itself powerfully evident. As they yielded themselves, God worked through them. Love is convicting. The tongues of fire were the language of God's love. They prompted a response.

I feel that so often our evangelism efforts are not genuinely salted with grace and love. We must learn to flow in what the Father is spontaneously speaking over any given situation. This is our own "tongues of fire," our own personal Pentecost. If we can speak what the Father is saying, His power will do the rest. People will hear heaven in their "own language," in a way that relates to them. We need to meet people where they are in their own spiritual journey. We need to learn how to relate. The gospel is about relational love.

Today in the Church, we can witness something that I call "ambush evangelism." This involves approaching strangers and quickly presenting the gospel in some formulaic way in order to "win a soul." This form of evangelism may include prophetic insights or words of encouragement that initially make people feel known and loved. Usually, after a little bit of passive pressure, people will agree to pray and "accept Jesus." There are usually smiles, a few high fives, and an overwhelming sense of accomplishment for all involved. The evangelists then go home, celebrate, and later talk about the experience as if some great spoils were won in a war.

---

[56] "The tongue also is a fire, a world of evil among the parts of the body. It corrupts the whole body, sets the whole course of one's life on fire, and it is itself set on fire by hell." James 3:6 (NIV)

I have been involved in this type of evangelism, but I honestly struggle with its fruit. Is a person better off for hearing the gospel in this manner? I am honestly not sure. Jesus may have actually commented on this type of "evangelism" when He said, *"Woe to you, teachers of the law and Pharisees, you hypocrites! You travel over land and sea to win a single convert, and when you have succeeded, you make them twice as much a child of hell as you are"* (Matthew 23:15, NIV). With these words, Jesus condemns religionists who are hell-bent on winning people over to mere ideologies. These "children of hell" fail to offer true and sustainable spiritual freedom. So often, I feel that our ambush evangelism does the same thing. Without proper follow-up teaching and a sound community, how can people actually learn about faith and grow in the reality of the new creation?

The Book of Acts provides a beautiful blueprint of new creation evangelism. Paul's apostolic work is a particular standout. Paul never seemed to pressure or force people into obedience to a religious structure. He was intent on sharing with the Jews the reality that the long-awaited kingdom of heaven, the hope of Israel, had finally arrived in and through the person of Jesus Christ.

After all, this reality had dramatically changed Paul. His powerful experience of the Savior's love overflowed naturally into evangelistic work. He spoke with a "tongue of fire," striving to meet people in their current place of understanding about God. A notable example of this is his speech before the philosophers at the Areopagus in Athens. Paul does not condemn these men for their beliefs or tell them they are believing the wrong thing. Instead, he validates their beliefs and leverages their worship by pointing it towards Jesus Christ. It is absolutely brilliant.

> "'Paul then stood up in the meeting of the Areopagus and said: "Men of Athens! I see that in every way you are very religious. For as I walked around and looked carefully at your objects of worship, I even found an altar with this inscription: TO AN UNKNOWN GOD. So you are ignorant of the very thing you worship… 'For in him we live and move and have our being.' As some of your own poets have said, 'We are his offspring.' Therefore since we are

God's offspring, we should not think that the divine being is like gold or silver or stone...he now commands all people everywhere to repent.'" Acts 17:22-30 (NIV)

In this passage, Paul masterfully meets the Greeks where they are in their understanding and points them toward a greater and truer reality that has dawned in the person of Jesus Christ. He even quotes a Greek poet to make his point. Some rejected the message, but some wanted to hear more. The fact remains that the gospel was presented as Paul leveraged a religious belief system that was already in place to speak the truth in love. The people then could decide their own response.

Like Paul, we need to learn to meet people where they are in their current understanding and perspective about God. We can then gently point them to the higher reality that we all have been invited to be a part of. If the truth that is presented in love is rejected, it is not our responsibility. As the Lord says, *"If anyone will not welcome you or listen to your words, leave that home or town and shake the dust off your feet"* (Matthew 10:14, NIV). Our responsibility is to present the message in peace.

The apostles never pressured anyone to accept the gospel. Rather, they encouraged people to *believe* the gospel. Whether we like it or not, a new reality (the new creation) is already making itself known and God has invited us all to become part of it, if we so wish. All men will eventually stand before God, whether they believe it or not.

The apostles' greatest opponents were not the common people, but the Jewish and pagan religious institutions and the political and financial powers associated with them. We need to rewire our thinking about evangelism and remove the blanket of fear that shrouds the Body of Christ. I contend that the gospel, if presented in love, is attractive to most people. What needs to change is our understanding and the way we present its timeless truths. No one pours new wine (the Holy Spirit's power) into old wineskins (fatigued religious understandings and presentations). New wine must be poured into new wineskins. New wineskins fit the needs of the age.[57]

If We Build It, They Will Come

So much of our evangelism today is motivated by the idea that the world as we know it could end at any given moment. The prevalent idea is that Jesus will come back on a cloud, the world will erupt in fire, and those who never accepted the gospel will be cast into a lake of sulphurous fire. Those who believe will be swept naked into the sky to meet the Lord in the air.

As has hopefully become clear from this book, this was not the perspective of the Bible writers, despite what popular "end times" verses may seem to superficially indicate. To reiterate: Jesus is God's rescue and renewal mission. God called creation "good" - He has no intention of destroying it. As you read this, the entire world is being actively remade (i.e. "re-created") into His image and likeness by the Holy Spirit. This is what is meant by the "appearing of the Lord" in the scriptures. We are called to participate in this reality with vision and patience, not believe godless myths that stoke fear and hinder our journey into the fullness of the kingdom.

The heart of new creation evangelism is the building of the new creation temple, which is the Body of Christ. Of course, we should feel compelled to rescue those who are perishing, but our eschatology (the way we approach the "end times") needs to evolve. As God's instrument for divine change on Earth, the Body of Christ is in it for the long haul. We are the new humanity who embody and transmit the realities of God's new creation. God is patient. It will take time for the kingdom to manifest its fullness - possibly hundreds or thousands of years. This is the source of our hope, and not only ours, but all of humanity's. The crux of this blessed hope is not that we will go to heaven instead of hell. Our hope is that God will fulfill His promise to rescue and redeem the entire cosmos from sin's infection, despite what present experience may seem to indicate.

---

[57] "No one sews a patch of unshrunk cloth on an old garment. Otherwise, the new piece will pull away from the old, making the tear worse. And no one pours new wine into old wineskins. Otherwise, the wine will burst the skins, and both the wine and the wineskins will be ruined. No, they pour new wine into new wineskins." Mark 2:21-22 (NIV)

The Old Testament prophets looked into the future and envisioned an "end times" temple that would cover the entire earth. As we learned in the introduction, we are this temple. As we grow in number, spiritual maturity and knowledge, the kingdom of God is made manifest through us and the "walls" of the new temple expand to fill the nations. The Body of Christ is *"the fullness of him who fills everything in every way"* (Ephesians 1:23, NIV).

Jesus instructs us to *"go and make disciples of all nations, baptizing them in the name of the Father and of the Son and of the Holy Spirit"* (Matthew 28:19, NIV). In this verse, the grammatical structure of the Greek implies *continuous* activity that happens as we go about our daily lives. It is about a lifestyle of God-immersion that radiates His presence into the lives of others, allowing them to see the Truth. As God's purified people, we are called to be zealous for good deeds. These good deeds are the works God has prepared in advance for us to walk in, works of love that advance the name of Jesus and the kingdom of heaven.

The prophets promise that as the Body of Christ grows in wisdom and stature and radiates the light of Christ, the nations of the world will flock to us:

> "In the last days the mountain of the Lord's temple will be established as the highest of the mountains; it will be exalted above the hills, and peoples will stream to it. Many nations will come and say, 'Come, let us go up to the mountain of the Lord, to the temple of the God of Jacob. He will teach us in his ways, so that we may walk in his paths.'" Micah 4:1-2, cf. Isaiah 2:2-3 (NIV)

> "'This is what the Lord Almighty says: "Many peoples and the inhabitants of many cities will yet come, and the inhabitants of one city will go to another and say, 'Let us go at once to entreat the Lord and seek the Lord Almighty. I myself am going.' And many peoples and powerful nations will come to Jerusalem (the Body of Christ) to seek the Lord Almighty and to entreat him...In those days ten people from all languages and nations will take firm hold of one [believer] by the hem of his robe and say, 'Let us go with

> you, because we have heard that God is with you.'" Zechariah 8:20-23 (NIV), parenthetical annotations mine
>
> "Arise, shine, for your light has come, and the glory of the Lord rises upon you. See, darkness covers the earth and thick darkness is over the peoples, but the Lord rises upon you and his glory appears over you. Nations will come to your light, and kings to the brightness of your dawn." Isaiah 60:1-3 (NIV)

The idea is that as we focus on building the glorious temple of God together, those outside of Christ will be drawn into belief. They will desire to experience what we experience with God. This may seem hard to believe right now because, if we are going on pure appearances, the Body of Christ doesn't look much different from the rest of the world. This is because in our current stage of spiritual development, our faith is still primarily intellectual. With the passage of time, as the faith matures from the intellectual to the intuitive and experiential, the differences will become more obvious. God's tangible presence and covenant blessings will become more and more evident in our experience as our corporate faith grows and increases. Our inheritance in the Spirit is a Promised Land that we are only just beginning to enter into.

We enter this spiritual Promised Land through the work of the apostles, prophets, evangelists, pastors, and teachers, who are sent by God for the building up of the Body of Christ. These spiritual "offices" direct the Body into the fullness of Christ's inheritance. They help us mature into the fullness of what has already been made available in Christ.

> "So Christ himself gave the apostles, the prophets, the evangelists, the pastors, and teachers, to equip his people for works of service, so that the body of Christ may be built up until we all reach unity in the faith and in the knowledge of the Son of God and become mature, attaining to the whole measure of the fullness of Christ." Ephesians 4:11-12 (NIV)

Remember, these "offices" in actuality are manifestations of the Holy Spirit that are given by God for the common good. Paul refers to these positions as "gifts" from Christ.[58] These manifestations of God's Spirit flow through people who have purified themselves from the ways of the old creation order:

> "Do your best to present yourself to God as one approved, a worker who does not need to be ashamed and who correctly handles the word of truth...In a large house there are articles not only of gold and silver, but also of wood and clay; some are for special purposes and some for common use. Those who cleanse themselves from [wickedness] will be instruments for special purposes, made holy, useful to the Master and prepared to do any good work." 2 Timothy 2:15, 20-21 (NIV)

We are the "articles" of God's "house." We all have a part to play in God's grand plan. I do not believe God's intentions for our lives are as fixed as we believe them to be. We know that no matter what, He has great plans for us. I believe that as we pursue righteousness, faith, love, and peace, He increases our sphere of influence in the Body and beyond. The way we manifest His presence evolves and changes as we grow in love and faith.

There will always be those who have a particular calling to go out and evangelize the world. These men and women are called missionaries. However, missionaries are not the only evangelists. We are all evangelists. The greatest thing we can do to evangelize is to love God and love our neighbor as ourselves. This is how God builds and expands His temple. It is the Father who ultimately draws men and women to Himself.[59] As we rest in Him and live in obedience, His power flowing through us opens the minds and hearts of unbelievers.

***

Evangelism is a core responsibility of God's anointed royal priesthood. New creation evangelism must first and foremost be a loving invitation into a glorious reality that we have the privilege of participating in. This glory is the

---

[58] See Ephesians 4:8.

[59] "No one can come to me (Jesus) unless the Father who sent me draws them, and I will raise them up at the last day." John 6:44 (NIV)

kingdom of heaven, which is the manifestation of God's reality. At the heart of evangelism is the expansion of God's new temple on earth, which is the Body of Christ.

Jesus Christ is our model and pattern for evangelism in the new creation. He presented the reality of the Father's kingdom with love and grace. This presentation of the kingdom was accompanied by miracles and wonders that affirmed the presence of heaven. Jesus had extraordinary evangelistic success by simply resting in the will of the Father and acting in obedience. As anointed priests, we are also called to follow Christ in this obedience.

Love meets people where they are in their current understanding and relationship with God. It condescends to establish relationship and connection. Jesus got down in the dirt with the women caught in adultery. He used gentle language but challenged her to become the person God had designed her to be.[60] By learning how to leverage the thoughts, attitudes, and experiences of others, we can show them that the Father is already present within them and working through their lives.

There is no need for our evangelism to be a strenuous effort. As we grow into personal and corporate maturity, the Body of Christ will radiate the love of the Father with greater and greater intensity. We are the light of the world, a city on a hill. The prophets promise us that the nations of the world will eventually stream to this light. Indeed, the knowledge of the glory of God has begun to cover the earth and millions have already come running into the arms of a loving Father.

---

[60] See John 8:3-11 for the story.

Part Three

Kings

We have now reached the final section of *New Creation Spirituality*. So far, we have examined our responsibilities as prophets and priests in the new creation. Undoubtedly, there is so much more that can be said about these roles beyond what has been presented in this text. This book is not intended as a systematic theology. It is an invitation to explore the realities of the new creation by examining the gospel from a different angle. It serves as an introduction to a refreshing new faith paradigm.

We are left with one more area of the anointing to explore: the kingly role of believers. Before we examine what it means to be a "king" in God's current reign, let's briefly review the dimensions of the anointing we have already explored. This is important because the three roles - prophet, priest and king - easily blend into each other. The functions of each of these offices inform and empower the others.

We first explored the prophetic anointing of believers. Prophets carry eternal life, which is the presence of Jesus Christ. They identify with God's heart for humanity and share His spiritual vision. Prophets live in a flow of revelation from the Father through the mind of Christ. By releasing God's presence, they bring heaven's reality to the earthly plane.

We then studied the priestly anointing of believers. Priests host, reflect, and manifest the presence of God by serving in His new temple, which is the Body of Christ. They offer their bodies as living sacrifices which God flows through to manifest His presence. The priestly anointing is characterized by prayer, worship, fellowship, and evangelism.

Lastly, we come to the office of anointed kings, for which I offer the following definition:

A king is an anointed individual who shares in the current rule and reign of Jesus Christ, wages spiritual warfare, and judges the world.

Without further ado, we will now dive into the kingly dimension of the anointing. It is my prayer that the truths we explore will dramatically alter your perspective on God's kingdom.

Chapter Nine

A New Kind of King

When I think of a king, I think of someone with great power, jurisdiction and influence. Kings have no superior or equal in their sphere of authority. History will readily tell us that there are good kings and there are bad kings. Good kings use the authority God has given them to bring justice, peace, and prosperity. Bad kings abuse power to exalt themselves at the expense of the common people. As Uncle Ben told Peter Parker in *Spiderman*, "With great power comes great responsibility." This is a truth that is not to be overlooked.

The kingly anointing gives us great power and authority in God's kingdom, but not the kind that you may immediately envision. Heaven's power and authority work much differently than earthly power and authority. Before examining our mandate to act as kings in God's kingdom, we need to first appreciate the kind of king Jesus was. It is impossible to understand our role as God's royalty without examining the nature of Christ's kingship. He is our model and pattern. *As He is, so are we in this world* (1 John 4:17, NKJV).

All Hail King Jesus

We must understand Jesus' kingship in the light of first-century Jewish Messianic expectation. At the time of Christ's coming, the Jews had long since been freed from their exile in Babylon and had returned to Israel, the

Promised Land. However, there was a glaring problem. In subjection to harsh Roman rule, the Jews were clearly not experiencing the fullness of peace, unity, prosperity and freedom that the prophets had promised would come to the people of God. But there was hope! The prophets had foreseen a conquering Messianic figure who would dramatically overthrow all oppression and restore the Israelite nation as the first and foremost amongst the world, as it had been under the rules of King David and King Solomon. The glory that once was would shine again for all the nations to see!

Enter Jesus Christ. The first-century Jews (with the exception of the Jesus movement, obviously) rejected Christ's ministry because He did not fit into their earthly expectations for a conquering Messiah. Instead of a mighty horse, He rode a lowly donkey. He wielded no sword, only words of grace and truth. He did not violently and dramatically overthrow the oppressive Roman regime. Instead, He was hung on a cross and killed by the very people He had come to save. So much for a conquering Messiah.

These events threw the first-century Jewish world into turmoil. During His time on earth, Jesus had gathered some disciples and began teaching that God's kingdom had arrived. "How could this be true given the natural state of Israel?" many Jews would have wondered. And yet, Jesus seemed to embody the characteristics of the Messiah that the prophets wrote of. Many Jews began to "believe in" Jesus. This belief was trust that He was indeed the Messiah who had come to fulfill and embody the promises of the Old Testament.

Belief in Jesus radically altered any pre-established understanding of the "kingdom of God." It wasn't a natural kingdom that God wanted to establish after all, but a spiritual one! Jesus had not just come to rescue and renew the Jewish people, but all of humanity! As such, everyone could now be included in the promises and eternal life of God. This truth infuriated the leaders of the Jewish religious system, long drunk on their religious pride and influence over the common people. In their fury and hatred, they began to persecute and kill the disciples of the emerging social-spiritual Jesus movement.

In Christianity, it is well known that Jesus Christ is God Himself. What is less understood is that Jesus is also a *revelation* of God. In other words, He *reveals* the character and nature of God the Father. As the "Word" of God, Jesus unveiled God's true character and nature. *"The Son is the radiance of God's glory and the exact representation of his being,"* the Bible states in Hebrews 1:3.

Jesus Christ reveals the perfect will of the Father. This will is not characterized by condemnation, anger, or disinterest. In and through Christ, God has revealed Himself as a God of pure love, intent on reconciling His lost children to Himself. Jesus and the Father do not have two separate wills, for they are of one mind and heart. *"Anyone who has seen me has seen the Father...Don't you believe that I am in the Father, and that the Father is in me...Believe me when I say that I am in the Father and the Father is in me,"* Jesus tells the disciples in John 14:10-11. If we want to understand the nature of the Father, Jesus is our model. If our ideas about God do not fit the character and nature of Christ, they are incorrect.

The point I want to establish here is that Jesus' priority was not to establish a natural kingdom, but a spiritual one. This is the revelation that the apostles and disciples were growing into and striving to steward. Christ's sacrifice was for both the Jews *and* the Gentiles. His death and resurrection created one new humanity out of two formerly distinct people groups.[61] This was always God's intention from the beginning - one family under heaven living in unity with each other and in union with God. *"My kingdom,"* Jesus told Pilate, *"is not of this world"* (John 18:36). Jesus came to institute a radical spirituality that stands in opposition to the existing worldly system of thinking and being.

The scriptures repeatedly emphasize that Jesus is "king" and "savior of the world." With these designations, the Bible writers were not just highlighting the fact that Jesus was the long-awaited Messianic king from the line of David. These phrases are employed so frequently in the New Testament because Caesar, the leader of the Roman Empire, also used these titles to describe himself. The Bible writers wanted to drive home the point that the true savior was not an earthly Caesar, but the heavenly Jesus. His kingdom does not consist of what can be seen. Paul tells us that the kingdom of God is *"not a matter of eating and drinking, but of righteousness, peace, and joy in the Holy Spirit"* (Romans 14:17, NIV). These are intangible, *spiritual* qualities.

---

[61] "For he himself is our peace, who has made the two groups one and has destroyed the barrier, the dividing wall of hostility, by setting aside in his flesh the law with its commands and regulations. His purpose was to create in himself one new humanity out of the two, thus making peace...for through him we both have access to the Father by one Spirit." Ephesians 2:14-17 (NIV)

Jesus now sits at the right hand of the Father in heaven and rules the entire universe. To "sit at the right hand" of the Father means that Jesus has absolute power and authority over everything seen and unseen. Jesus sits *"far above all rule and authority, power, and dominion, and every name that is invoked, not only in the present age but also in the one to come. And God has placed all things under his feet and appointed him to be head over everything for the church, which is his body, the fullness of him who fills everything in every way,"* Paul writes in Ephesians 1:21-22.

The scriptures tell us Christ reigns over both heaven and earth. *"All authority in heaven and on earth has been given to me,"* Jesus tells the disciples in Matthew 28:18. This is a wonderful reality, but there is an elephant left standing in the room. If Jesus truly rules and reigns as king of the universe, why do we not see this reality manifest in our experience?

How we choose to answer this question defines our Christian hope. For years, I had believed the answer to this was that Jesus wants more people to be "saved" and is therefore waiting to consummate the fullness of His kingdom. Someday, hopefully soon, Jesus will "come back" and destroy/re-make an evil world with the fire of heaven. Believers will be given eternal life and non-believers will be thrown into hell. Until then, we need to hold onto "faith" and just wait for heaven to act on our behalf. This Christian worldview is known in literary terms as a *deux ex machina*. A *deus ex machina* is an event in fiction or drama in which a person or thing suddenly and dramatically appears to rescue characters out of a seemingly hopeless, unsolvable situation.

The *deus ex machina* perspective is a far cry from the worldview of the apostles. Jesus is not "waiting" for the right moment to come back and "fix the world." The cross was the judgment on the old creation order - not on people, but on the sin, death, and forces of evil that oppressed humanity. John 3:17 tells us that *"God did not send His Son into the world to condemn the world, but to save the world through him."* To "save" the world is to redeem and restore it to match God's divine design. When God created the world, He called it *good*. His thoughts have not somehow changed because of humanity's sinful condition. We are called to partner with the ascended Christ in His mission to renew and restore the cosmos from sin's infection.

We do not yet see the fullness of Christ's victory for one simple reason: God is love. He cannot violate His essential character and nature, which is love.

He is love, joy, peace, patience, kindness, goodness, faithfulness, gentleness, and self-control. Love is long-suffering. God's power is based in and derived from His love. His kingdom advances through love. We are the agents of His love, His ministers of reconciliation.[62] A lost humanity cannot be forced into loving God. We must willfully *choose* Him. This is what fulfills the law of love.

Imagine a scenario in which Christ suddenly and unexpectedly rides in on a cloud to reshape the earth with "unquenchable" fire, effectively ending time as we know it. In this instance, what does logic dictate would happen to humanity's free choice? It would cease to exist because the ascended Christ has entered the natural realm to impose His sovereign will on all of humanity. Our free choice would disappear instantly. This does not align with the character and nature of Jesus, who is love itself. Love cannot impose itself, nor will it ever. As long as we are alive, humans have access to free choice. Without free choice, there is no love because the two are inextricably linked. If Christ were to actually do something like this, we would all instantly become God's robots. Unfortunately, many Christians have been taught that this is exactly what Christ's Second Coming will look like. It is important to understand that God's sovereignty doesn't change the fact that He is love itself. Everything He does is motivated by love. Christ's Second Coming will occur when humanity as a whole chooses God in love.

God's kingdom advances through one essential means: love. Love actively sustains and upholds the entire universe. It is the very atmosphere of heaven. God's kingdom is Christ's reign of love. He has invited us to be a part of this kingdom that has already arrived and now continues to make itself known.

Servant Kings

As God's anointed kings, we are active participants in the current reign of Jesus Christ. We rule alongside Him. The book of Revelation tells us that God has made us to be *"kings who serve God and reign on earth"* (Revelation 5:10). Paul writes in Romans that we will reign *in* life through Jesus Christ, having

---

[62] God was reconciling the world to himself in Christ, not counting people's sins against them. And he has committed to us the message of reconciliation. We are therefore Christ's ambassadors..." 2 Corinthians 5:19-20 (NIV)

received an abundant provision of grace and righteousness.[63] To "reign" in God's kingdom is not to wield power or influence over others. To reign with Christ is to serve and, ultimately, suffer with Him in order to advance the kingdom. Heavenly reigning is the opposite of earthly reigning. The kings of heaven are its greatest servants.

Christ reveals that the power of heaven flows through sacrificial love and acts that accord with this love. God's power is His love. John writes that *"greater love has no one than this: to lay down one's life for one's friends"* (John 15:13, NIV). The Messiah is the revelation that God's power is revealed in human weakness, not strength. Christ is not an earthly king. He does not subjugate others to His will through force or power. He presents Himself through love and allows others to decide how to respond to this love.

Christ lived obedient to the Father's will, even to the point of death. Although being in very nature God, He did not place much stock in His equality with the Father. As God's imagers, those made in His likeness and filled with His heavenly authority, we are called to do the same. Heavenly glory and exaltation arise from sacrifice and servitude. This is wildly contrary to the pattern of this dark age that is already passing away. To continually abide in humility and servitude are the great challenges of Christian spirituality.

> "In your relationships with one another, have the same mindset as Christ Jesus: Who, being in very nature God, did not consider equality with God something to be used to his own advantage; rather, he made himself nothing by taking the nature of a servant, being made in human likeness. And being found in the appearance as a man, he humbled himself by becoming obedient to death - even death on a cross!" Philippians 2:5-9 (NIV)

The primary ethic of the kingdom is love and service. We "rule" with Christ by loving our enemies and laying down our lives in service to God and others. We "reign with Christ" as we empty ourselves of our ego and selfish desires. This is our spiritual process and our internal battle. As we lay ourselves down,

---

[63] "For if, by the trespass of the one man, death reigned through that one man, how much more will those who receive God's abundant provision of grace and of the gift of righteousness **reign in life** through the one man, Jesus Christ!" Romans 5:17 (NIV)

God's spiritual power is made manifest in and through the natural realm. This is God's glory, the kingdom revealed!

This is where suffering comes into the picture. Suffering is the natural result of surrendering our whole selves to others and to God for the sake of His kingdom. It is the cost of absolute obedience. There will be suffering as we surrender everything within us that belongs to the old creation order. This requires steadfastness and patience in the face of external and internal oppositions or obstacles. Love for Christ and His kingdom sets us in opposition to the patterns of the old creation order and the humans who worship these patterns. As the old creation clashes with the new, conflicts naturally arise.

I used to think suffering for the gospel meant adopting a stoic and morose spirituality. I equated spiritual suffering with poverty, martyrdom, persecution, and joylessness. I believed that if I never experienced these things, I could never be a real Christian. Deep down, I believed Christianity only existed to help us survive the horrors and darkness of the world. I had no present hope. The little hope I did have was for the distant future. One day, Jesus would arrive and free me from my deep internal misery. These were all religious lies that I had come to believe were true. As Jesus freed me from my delusion, I began to consider suffering in an entirely new light.

Christian suffering is not to be characterized by doom and gloom, but indescribable joy. The writer of Hebrews tells us that Jesus endured the cross because of the joy that was set before Him![64] Jesus realized that His obedience would manifest the kingdom in indescribable measure. Paul had clearly realized this revelation when he wrote, *"We do not lose heart...our light and momentary troubles are achieving for us an eternal glory that far outweighs them all"* (2 Corinthians 4:17, NIV). For Paul, this "glory" wasn't some shadowy reward in the afterlife, but the reality that Christ would manifest His presence in and through Paul as a result of his trials. If our suffering is producing hopelessness in our hearts, we need to pray and ask God for His mind on the matter. Obedience and steadfastness in suffering manifests the kingdom. The kingdom is the manifest presence of the Holy Spirit. If we can get our

---

[64] "Let us run with perseverance the race marked out for us, fixing our eyes on Jesus, the pioneer and perfecter of faith. For the joy set before him he endured the cross, scorning its shame, and sat down at the right hand of the throne of God." Hebrews 12:1-2 (NIV)

perspective off ourselves and onto the bigger picture, we will be able to find joy in whatever we may face. There is nothing worse than a Christian whose worldview is colored by negativity and defeat.

Our suffering, which comes in all shapes, sizes, and varieties, is mitigated by the reality of God's presence operating within and through us. Suffering is painful for many Christians because they are missing a piece of the puzzle - God's manifest presence. It is God's presence that turns suffering to joy and creates beauty from ashes. Paul writes in Ephesians 1:3 that *"God has blessed us in the heavenly realms with every spiritual blessing in Christ Jesus."* These blessings are spiritual graces that aid us in our call to suffer/reign with Christ. God has fully equipped us with the blessings of heaven so that we may stand firm in the face of suffering. Nothing is wasted in the kingdom – all things work for the good of those who love God.

Jesus told His disciples, *"I have given you authority to trample on snakes and scorpions and to overcome all the power of the enemy; nothing will harm you"* (Luke 10:19, NIV). All authority in heaven and on earth has been given to Christ, and He has bestowed this authority on humanity for the advancing of the kingdom of heaven. This authority is what allows us to confront our enemies and suffer with boldness and confidence.

Christ's Triumphal Procession

We can now more fully address the question I posed earlier: If Jesus has already won the victory, why don't we see it in our experience? What is preventing the kingdom from manifesting in its fullness? Why do we still experience sin, sickness, strife, and death? The simple answer to these questions is that humanity remains shrouded in unbelief. Remember, God is love. He cannot force Himself or His kingdom into or onto the children whom He loves. We must choose Him. Love is the essence of the kingdom.

The unbelief of humanity is empowered by the spiritual forces of wickedness in the unseen realm. These entities resonate with and oppress the hearts and minds of humans who are in bondage to spiritual idolatry. Remember, Christ came to inaugurate a *spiritual* kingdom. The realities of this kingdom play out in the unseen realm. Christ's earthly ministry brought strong opposition from these spiritual forces. They are known throughout the New Testament as demons, evil spirits, the devil, and Satan. Jesus makes it quite clear that His lost children are not His enemies. His true opponents are the spiritual forces that oppress humanity and drive wicked behavior. Human cooperation with evil is what empowers its existence and ability to thrive.

We must adopt the way of thinking that has been presented throughout this book: Heaven and earth are not separate entities that exist independently of each other. They are two realms of experience and existence that operate in tandem. One reality is spiritual, the other is earthly. The spiritual is unseen, the earthly is seen. Spiritual realities become evident from what can be observed on the earthly plane. We must think in two dimensions at once. This is a hard concept to grasp in an age of scientific rationalism, but it is a truth clearly presented in the New Testament.

What is important to understand is that we are not in some sort of cosmic battle in which good and evil are two equal and opposing forces. The cross has already provided the victory for all of mankind, for all of eternity. What is left is an *awakening* to the reality of the finished work of the cross. Christ's finished work is the foundation of the new creation. As we come to believe in Christ and share in His Holy Spirit, the forces of evil are disempowered and neutralized. This is the gospel. When we come alive to the revelation of our union with Christ, bondages are broken, and darkness flees. The enemy has already been defeated. Humans not awakened to this reality will continue to experience oppression and evil.

When Christ died on the cross, resurrected, and sent His Spirit to humanity, He gave to us a gift of union with Him. Our loving union with Him is the weapon He uses to cleanse the world of sin and evil. Paul makes the analogy that we are now on a victory march into heaven behind Christ, the ascended King. The reluctant spectators of this march are the disempowered forces of evil who cannot bear Christ's glorified presence within us:

> "But thanks be to God, who always leads us as captives in Christ's triumphal procession and uses us to spread the aroma of the knowledge of him everywhere. For we are to God the pleasing aroma of Christ among those who are being saved and those who are perishing. To the one we are

an aroma that brings death; to another, an aroma that brings life." 2 Corinthians 2:14-16 (NIV)

"God made us alive with Christ. Having forgave us all our sins... cancelling the charge of our legal indebtedness, which stood against us and condemned us; he has taken it away, nailing it to the cross. And having disarmed the powers and authorities, he made a public spectacle of them, triumphing over them by the cross." Colossians 2:13-15 (NIV)

Our mission as servant-kings is to rescue other humans who still live bound to the spiritual forces of wickedness, be it through ignorance, delusion, or the willful rejection of God's love. Our weapons are the love and truth of Jesus Christ. Like Christ, we are called to present the love of God with grace. This is a core component of the gospel. It is God's desire to use us powerfully in the natural and spiritual realms simultaneously:

"I (Paul) became a servant of this gospel by the gift of God's grace given me through the working of his power...to preach to the Gentiles the boundless riches of Christ...**His intent was that now, through the church, the manifold wisdom of God should be made known to the rulers and authorities in the heavenly realms**, according to his eternal purpose that he accomplished in Christ Jesus our Lord." Ephesians 3:7-11 (NIV)

Our call to serve as kings is a call to love. As we strive to love God and others, we can be sure we will encounter opposition from the forces of evil that operate through the hearts of those who do not know Christ. This is where we are called to hard obedience. It is through this obedience in the face of suffering that the realities of God's kingdom become manifest in greater and greater measure. In the end, divine love will win.

A Lesson from Corinth

It is an incredible reality that God desires to use us here on earth to accomplish His divine purposes. We must remember that our status as God's anointed kings is first and foremost a call to surrender, love and humility.

With great power comes great responsibility. If we are not careful, our free access to God's power can create serious problems.

We can learn many important lessons from the ancient church in Corinth. It is clear from both 1 Corinthians and 2 Corinthians that the believers there had difficulties stewarding the power and authority that God had freely given them. As they began to prioritize God's giftings and manifestations over love and humility, sin found an open door. The Corinthian church was prone to division, sexual immorality, and histrionic spiritual manifestation.[65] The Corinthians carried an unhealthy view of spirituality and divine kingship. They placed the cart before the horse. Paul sarcastically chides them for their incorrect understanding of the kingly anointing:

> "For who makes you different from anyone else? What do you have that you did not receive? And if you did receive it, why do you boast as though you did not? Already you have become rich! You have begun to reign - and that without us! How I wish that you really had begun to reign so that we also might reign with you!...We are fools for Christ, but you are so wise in Christ! We are weak, but you are strong! You are honored, we are dishonored!" 1 Corinthians 4:7-10 (NIV)

Today, it is common to improperly reference passages from Corinthians to downplay or demonize manifestations of the Holy Spirit. I think the modern Church tends to misunderstand the root of the issues in Corinth. There is nothing wrong with having a Christian spirituality that prioritizes our righteous status as God's sons and daughters and the manifestations of the Holy Spirit. The issue is when these components of the gospel end up overshadowing unity in the Body of Christ. What matters is cohesion in God's divine family. God's presence is designed to empower unity, not destroy it.

The spiritual giftings that come from our righteous status as the sons of God are for the building up of the Body of Christ, as we explored in Part 2 of this book. They enable us to serve each other and humanity in partnership with God's empowering presence. Serving humanity will sometimes mean

---

[65] See 1 Corinthians 1:10-17, 1 Corinthians 6:12-20, and 1 Corinthians 12.

suffering and sacrificing our concept of "self." This is where we must learn to lean on the power of God.

I remember when I first learned about the fullness of God's kingdom and began to access the gifts and graces of the Holy Spirit. As God began to bless me with wisdom and revelation, I also started to flow in prophetic words for people, healing, and other unusual miracles. The thrill of all of this does something to a man, no matter how pure our intentions may be. I began to subtly look down on other believers for what I perceived to be a lack (and even rejection) of true Christian belief. Everyone needed to experience what I was experiencing! I figured that if others wanted to live in the freedom I was enjoying, they would need to start making some spiritual effort, like I was. Rather than loving people in their current level of knowledge and revelation, I belittled them in my heart and mind. I had fallen prone to Corinthian sin. This is perhaps the greatest temptation when the Holy Spirit really begins to flow through us.

On the opposite end of the spectrum is the rejection of the manifestation of the Holy Spirit. This is equally as prideful and deadly as Corinthian hyper-spirituality (*"Do not quench the Spirit!"* Paul warns in 1 Thessalonians 5:19). In my Christian walk, I have spent time living in both camps. Christians intent on quenching the Spirit are like skeletons who walk around in churches with Bibles chained to their hands. There is little desire or motivation for a deeper experience of the Spirit. The faith is a mere intellectual trophy that gets lorded over others. This is religionism. It is a lifeless ghost that masquerades as a living being.

The kings of heaven are the servants of man. I believe the greatest heroes of heaven are people we have never heard of - men and women who quietly and faithfully stewarded the servant heart of Jesus Christ during their time on earth. Today, we have a tendency to think that someone's public visibility equates with their spiritual authority. This generates a kind of Christian celebrity culture. This was also clearly a problem in the Corinthian church:

> "My brothers and sisters, some from Chloe's household have informed me that there are quarrels among you. What I mean is this: One of you says, 'I follow Paul'; another, 'I

follow Apollos'; another, 'I follow Peter'; still another, 'I follow Christ.'" 1 Corinthians 1:11-12 (NIV)

Those in the public eye are not any more blessed than those who are not. We all have a significant role to play in God's kingdom - He does not show favoritism. Public prominence means nothing in heaven. Packing your child's lunchbox with the love of Christ is just as important to God as packing stadiums with people who love Christ. All of us have full access to the Spirit of God, a point Paul makes clear to the Corinthians:

> "So then, no more boasting about human leaders! All things are yours, whether Paul or Apollos or Peter or the world or life or death or the present or the future - all are yours, and you are of Christ, and Christ is of God." 1 Corinthians 3:21-32 (NIV)

"Promotion" in the Body of Christ has nothing to do with gaining positions of influence or authority. If God gives us these things, they are only a means to better love and serve the people who are around us. The old creation humanity craves influence over others because it offers a false sense of power and security. This is the pattern of the world - it is evil. True heavenly promotion is God offering us opportunities in which we can be more useful to others.

God has already given us everything in heaven. We will find that as we begin to love others and use the graces God gives us to do so, He will empower us with even more of His presence. Love is power in the kingdom of God. Everything we do must flow through a filter of genuine love and concern for others. It is a journey and a learning experience. We walk with the Lord so that we can learn how to love others in the same manner that He loves us. This is what it means to be a king.

***

In this chapter, I introduced the kingly anointing of believers. Having been united with Christ, we are invited into His rule and reign. This reign is a reign of love. Christ did not come to establish an earthly kingdom, but a spiritual one. This spiritual kingdom is known in the scriptures as the "Body of Christ" and the "New Jerusalem." This kingdom is not defined by earthly parameters such as geography, social class, or race. We are all one in Christ.

Jesus is our model and pattern for the kingly anointing. Our kingly call is to love and serve others, even to the point of death. Christ did not consider His union with God as something to be lorded over others for His own sake. Rather, He became obedient to the Father for the sake of love, even to the point of death. This obedience radically restructured reality in both the spiritual and earthly realms. The Son now holds power and authority in both of these realms. The life of Christ reveals that obedience in the face of suffering manifests the kingdom of God.

Jesus disarmed the forces of evil on the cross by uniting humanity to Himself. He destroyed the rules and regulations that impeded a living relationship with Him. He has given us His Spirit. Through the Spirit, we are called to engage with the forces of evil in the heavenly realms who continue to influence and oppress humanity. Our weapons are love, grace and truth.

Spiritual pride can blind us from serving God and others in humility and devotion. God's anointed kings have access to the manifest riches of the heavenly realms. These riches empower us to serve others and build the kingdom of God. As we grow in genuine love, God increases our sphere of influence on earth so we may better serve others and advance His kingdom.

Chapter Ten

This Means War

We learned in the previous chapter that God's anointed kings share in the reign of Christ by suffering alongside Him. This suffering is not some sort of spiritual self-loathing or willful penance. Suffering is a natural consequence of living between the age that is passing away and the age of the new creation. It is the spiritual fire that results as God burns away everything that does not belong in His kingdom. At the center of all suffering is spiritual warfare.

A core conviction I now hold is that the kingdom of God cannot manifest externally until it is realized internally. To "realize" the kingdom is to *become* the Word of God, to embody Christ in ever-increasing measure. We cannot manifest the kingdom in our actions until its realities dominate our hearts. I believe Paul had this in mind when he wrote, *"And we all, who with unveiled faces contemplate the Lord's glory, are being transformed into his image with ever-increasing glory, which comes from the Lord, who is the Spirit"* (2 Corinthians 3:18, NIV). The realization and manifestation of the kingdom occur on both the personal and corporate levels. As we individually strive for and realize the kingdom, the corporate Body of Christ is also affected.

The scriptures show us that we must go through many hardships to enter the kingdom of God.[66] These hardships are connected to our spiritual battles. The paradox is that we have all been called into a spiritual war that has already been won. Jesus defeated evil once and for all on the cross. What is left is humanity awakening to this reality. In this chapter, we will explore how spiritual warfare is the means by which we awaken to God's fullness.

Principalities and Powers

"Our struggle is not against flesh and blood, but against the rulers, against the authorities, against the powers of this dark world and the spiritual forces of evil in the heavenly realms," Paul writes in Ephesians 6:12. This is a familiar passage to many. Who or what are these mysterious powers that Paul writes about? Where did they come from? Are they fallen angels? Disembodied spirits of the dead? Lanky red goat-men who carry pitchforks?

Depending on who you talk to, you may hear many different answers to these questions. What is pertinent for us to understand and what becomes very evident from the scriptures is that the apostles and disciples understood that they had a spiritual adversary, known in the New Testament as Satan or "the devil." Jesus Christ came to expose and destroy the works of this devil.[67] This devil is also described by Paul as the *"ruler of the kingdom of the air, the spirit who is now at work in those who are disobedient"* (Ephesians 2:2, NIV). Satan, therefore, is to be understood as a spiritual force who flows through humans to oppose the kingdom of God. That's all we need to know.

We don't need a degree in demonology (yes, they exist) to contend with the spiritual forces of wickedness. God hasn't called us to dwell on evil or waste our time in speculation. Evil spirits and demons are but shadows, empowered and strengthened by human belief. They exist and oppress humanity because the human heart has left a place for them. It is our spiritual idolatry that invites this influence and oppression.

---

[66] e.g. Acts 14:21-22 (NIV) "They preached the gospel in that city and won a large number of disciples. Then they returned to Antioch, strengthening the disciples and encouraging them to remain true to the faith. 'We must go through many hardships to enter the kingdom of God,' they said."

[67] "The one who does what is sinful is of the devil, because the devil has been sinning from the beginning. The reason the Son of God appeared was to destroy the devil's work." 1 John 3:7-8 (NIV)

The human heart and mind are the channels through which the spiritual realm manifests into the natural realm. Spiritual realities play out on the earthly plane. The problem is that modern Christianity tends to downplay and even ignore the idea that a spiritual realm exists in conjunction with our realm. Instead, we think of spiritual things as being in the "beyond" or "out there somewhere." This harms us much more than we may realize. The spiritual realm and the natural realm have always existed in codependent interconnection. Christ reminds of us this truth.

Paul writes, *"the god of this age has blinded the minds of unbelievers, so that they cannot see the light of the gospel that displays the glory of Christ, who is the image of God"* (2 Corinthians 4:4, NIV). Paul's focus here is the human heart and mind. He emphasizes spiritual blindness. This blindness is a spiritual ignorance that results in wicked behavior and cooperation with evil.

Believers have not been left to grope about in the dark. Christ has shone His light into our hearts so that we may know and access a greater reality - heaven's way of thinking and being. We have the mind of Christ and the heart of the Father. This Christ-light allows us to walk in truth, purity, and righteousness. Our "battle" plays out in the unseen. It is a war of ideas - divine truth against carnal reasoning, godly knowledge against delusion and falsity, light against dark. Our spiritual enemies lose influence when the false beliefs that empower them are confronted and deconstructed.

> "We live in the world, but we do not wage war as the world does. The weapons we fight with are not the weapons of the world. On the contrary, they have divine power to demolish strongholds. We demolish arguments and every pretension that sets itself up against the knowledge of God, and we take captive every thought and make it obedient to Christ." 2 Corinthians 10:4-5 (NIV)

This passage from 2 Corinthians is brilliant because it subtly draws a metaphor between the Israelites entering the Promised Land and New Covenant believers entering the fullness of the kingdom of God. The ancient Israelite kings fought against flesh and blood with tangible weapons. God's New Covenant anointed kings, the Body of Christ, fight spiritual enemies with spiritual weapons. These spiritual weapons are truthful speech and the power of God, which are *"weapons of righteousness in the right hand and in the left"* (2 Corinthians 6:7). "Strongholds" are entrenched patterns of thinking that belong to the old creation order. As they are demolished through spiritual process, the kingdom of God and the reality of the new creation is made manifest within us.

Just as God is eternal and limitless, so is His kingdom. We do not need to wait for death to access and experience the limitless realities of heaven. As we wage spiritual warfare and allow the Holy Spirit to reform our hearts and minds, we enter into God's spiritual Promised Land. God's new creation humanity embodies and manifests the treasure that is to be found there. It is an inheritance of glory.

Demolishing Strongholds and Killing Giants

Strongholds, patterns of thinking unaligned to the reality of the new creation, are demolished through spiritual process. God seeks to transform both individuals and humanity as a whole into a purified expression of His image and likeness. This process will not happen overnight. His work within us as individuals will go on for our entire lives and possibly even beyond. For the Body of Christ and humanity at large, it will continue for many generations.

The dynamics of our spiritual process could occupy many books. I introduce a theology for it and give an overview of the process in my first book, *The Mind of Christ: Christian Identity in the New Creation*. What is found in this chapter is a condensed version of the truths I outline there. We must understand that our salvation from the Lord is a progressive renewal and restoration of the human spirit to match the reality of the indwelling Christ. To be conformed into a more perfect expression of Christ is to become fully human. This is because God gradually restores us to match the blueprint of our original design, who is Christ.[68]

Salvation is continual and constant renewal. It isn't something to be received in the intellect and then set aside. Treating salvation in this way is like borrowing a book from God that we never open. Eventually, it gets lost

---

[68] "Through him all things were made; without him nothing was made that has been made. In him was life, and that life was the light of all mankind." John 1:3-4 (NIV)

somewhere in our library. Sometime later, God comes looking for it. We know we have it but have no idea where it is. I feel like this is how many of us treat our Christian faith today.

The first step in our spiritual process is to attain fundamental knowledge about Christ. This comes by receiving teaching from the Word that informs us of proper Christian doctrine, the essentials of salvation, and the basics of living a godly life in the world. This is what I refer to as the "intellectual" faith. It's important, but intellectual truths about God can only take us so far into the Spirit. We are called beyond the merely intellectual into the intuitive and experiential. Faith that is solely intellectual is referred to adversely by Jesus Christ in the parable of the sower:

> "'A farmer (Christ) went out to sow his seed (salvation)...Some fell on rocky places (intellectualism), where it did not have much soil (genuine love for God). It sprang up quickly, because the soil was shallow. But when the sun (trials and temptations) came up, the plants (our spirits) were scorched, and they withered because they had no root...'" Matthew 13:3-6 (NIV), parenthetical annotations mine

Intellectual faith does not produce deep roots of trust in the human heart. It is only an open door that allows us to access the reality of God's love. Intellectual faith without a deeper experience of God and His love only serves to puff us up and fill us with a false sense of superiority. Our intellectual faith is therefore only a foundation upon which God plans to build a glorious home for His presence. This glorious house is an unshakable relationship with Him, despite any opposing internal or external circumstances. God's goal is to move us all progressively from a merely intellectual faith into an intuitive and experiential one. As the Word is "made flesh" in each of us, we progressively experience the world in the same way that Jesus does and become certain of divine realities. Everything we do becomes energized by His higher reality.

God matures our faith by allowing trials and tribulations, which come in all sorts of shapes, sizes, and varieties. Trials and tribulations are both external and internal. External trials occur in our natural circumstances. They may be persecutions, financial difficulties, or issues with our health. External trials encourage us to turn our attention toward God and to rely on the promises that He outlines in the Word. They are recalibrating for our spiritual life and allow us to reset our priorities. They are opportunities for us to trust God in a deeper, more tangible way.

The highest external trial is martyrdom. Martyrs suffer for the faith to the point of death. In doing so, they illuminate the kingdom for others to see. The death of a martyr releases power in the heavenly realms. When Jesus died, the dead bodies of many holy people were raised to life, came out of their tombs, and went into Jerusalem to appear before many people.[69]

The challenge of external trials is that they oftentimes happen at the hands of other human beings. It is these moments that truly test our love. Jesus said, *"Love your enemies and pray for those who persecute you. If you love those who love you, what reward will you get?"* (Matthew 5:44-46, NIV). I cannot imagine the pain that God feels knowing that His beloved children choose to attack and kill one another in both word and deed. We must consider Christ, who came to His own with love and truth and yet was killed for it. What drove Him was the great victory that His death would achieve for all of humanity: the inauguration of the kingdom of God. This same mindset must inform our thinking when we suffer unjustly at the hands of others. Nothing that is done in love will be forgotten by the Lord. Every act of genuine love advances the kingdom. Sooner or later, all who do evil will be held to account by God for their wicked works.

Internal trials are those that assault the human mind. They are known in the scriptures as "temptations." Temptations occur when old creation thinking patterns ("strongholds") surface and release through their gates tormenting thoughts and anxieties ("giants"). The ancient Israelite spies were fearful when they found giants occupying the Promised Land.[70] Our spiritual giants are personal fears and torments empowered by false beliefs concerning our identity in Christ. Internal trials bring us face to face with the principalities and powers and the forces of wickedness in the heavenly realms.

---

[69] "At that moment the curtain of the temple was torn in two from top to bottom. The earth shook, the rocks split and the tombs broke open. The bodies of many holy people who had died were raised to life. They came out of the tombs after Jesus' resurrection and went into the holy city and appeared to many people." Matthew 27:51-53 (NIV)

[70] See Numbers 13:33.

These trials are overcome through suffering, in which we learn to surrender our minds and hearts completely to the Holy Spirit. We must boldly face our fears with the truths of God's Word and the power of the Holy Spirit. As we grow in a deeper spiritual revelation of our identity in Christ, spiritual giants are slain, and strongholds are demolished. The prophet Amos says of the Holy Spirit: *"With a blinding flash he destroys the stronghold and brings the fortified city to ruin"* (Amos 5:9, NIV). This "blinding flash" is personal enlightenment that the Holy Spirit gives to us as we wage war against darkness and demolish personal strongholds.

External and internal trials are forms of suffering. Suffering builds the kingdom within us through the application of spiritual pressure. Muscle can't grow unless it is utilized and torn apart through exercise. The kingdom cannot grow within us if we are never put to the test or remain in faulty thinking about our identity in Christ. God's anointed kings have been empowered with the Holy Spirit for spiritual trials that build the kingdom.

The epistles of the New Testament comment extensively on suffering. James tells us that perseverance in the face of suffering will produce the "crown of life." Crowns are worn by royalty. God's anointed kings *are* royalty. The crown of life is the mind of Christ - His way of thinking and being.

> "Blessed is the one who perseveres under trial because, having stood the test, that person will receive the crown of life that the Lord has promised to those who love him." James 1:12 (NIV)

Peter writes that suffering frees us from sinful thinking patterns and produces glory within us. Glory is the manifestation of the kingdom of God:

> "Therefore, since Christ suffered in His body, arm yourselves also with the same attitude, because whoever suffers in the body is done with sin...Dear friends, do not be surprised at the fiery ordeal that has come on you to test you, as though something strange were happening to you. But rejoice inasmuch as you participate in the sufferings of

Christ, so that you may be overjoyed when his glory is revealed." 1 Peter 4:1,12-13 (**NIV**)

"You greatly rejoice, though now for a little while you may have had to suffer grief in all kinds of trials. These have come so that the proven genuineness of your faith - of greater worth than gold, which perishes even though refined by fire - may result in praise, glory, and honor when Christ is revealed." 1 Peter 1:6-7 (**NIV**)

And, of course, Paul was no stranger to suffering. It is evident from his life and letters that he carried a robustly positive view of suffering:

"We are hard pressed on every side, but not crushed; perplexed, but not in despair; persecuted, but not abandoned; struck down, but not destroyed. We always carry around in our body the death of Jesus, so that the life of Jesus may also be revealed in our body." 2 Corinthians 4:8-10 (**NIV**)

"Let us boast in the hope of the glory of God. Not only so, but let us glory in our sufferings, because we know that suffering produces perseverance; perseverance, character; and character, hope." Romans 5:3-5 (**NIV**)

"Now if we are children, then we are heirs - heirs of God and co-heirs with Christ, if indeed we share in his sufferings in order that we may also share in his glory. I consider that our present sufferings are not worth comparing with the glory that will be revealed in us. For the creation waits in eager expectation for the children of God to be revealed." Romans 8:15-17 (**NIV**)

We can see a mutual theme unites these passages from the scriptures: perseverance in the face of suffering produces glory, which is the manifest reality of God's kingdom. Victory in spiritual warfare disarms the wicked principalities and powers and fills us with light, grace, and truth. Suffering awakens us to the reality of what has already been accomplished by Jesus on the cross, which is the fullness of the kingdom of God. This is what informed Paul's words when he wrote: *"I want to know Christ - yes, to know the power of his resurrection and participation in his sufferings, becoming like him in his death, and so, somehow, attaining to the resurrection from the dead"* (Philippians 3:10, NIV).

Revelation's Seven Promises

God's anointed kings are called to live in the victory of Jesus Christ. God makes some extraordinary promises to those who overcome trials, temptations, and tribulations. Many of these promises are laid out by the apostles in their epistles, but I want to take time to highlight some biblical promises I think are of particular significance. When we catch a vision for what can become possible through spiritual victory, our lives change forever. God rewards those who seek Him. We do not need to wait for life in the veiled beyond to enjoy the fruits of our obedience to Christ.

The book of Revelation was written by the apostle John to seven different churches, all of which were facing intense persecution. In this book, Jesus Christ prophetically encourages and challenges these churches. Jesus makes promises to those who overcome in each church. There are seven promises for seven churches. Anyone familiar with Hebrew symbology will recognize that the number seven speaks of divinity, wholeness, and God's perfection. Revelation is a prophetic book written in a prophetic style. It is full of metaphor, symbolism, and allusion. To understand Christ's seven promises, we must adopt a lens of interpretation that honors John's writing style. If we can do this, we will enjoy the book's rich spiritual treasury.

Promise 1: The Tree of Life (Ephesus)

> "Whoever has ears, let them hear what the Spirit says to the churches. To the one who is victorious, I will give the right to eat from the tree of life, which is in the paradise of God."
> Revelation 2:7-8 (NIV)

Here, the victorious are given the right to "eat from the tree of life, which is in the paradise of God." This verse is an allusion to the ancient Garden of Eden, where mankind lived immersed in the presence of God. This particular tree is not literal, of course. The "tree of life" is Jesus Christ, who rules and reigns from God's realm and allows us to partake of His eternal life. His fruit is the fruit of the Spirit - love, joy, peace, patience, kindness, gentleness, goodness, faithfulness, and self-control - and the graces of the Spirit, which are spiritual giftings and abilities. All of these things are manifestations of the kingdom of God. As we gain spiritual victory, God awakens us to the fullness of His giftings and graces. They become increasingly more tangible and manifest in our experience.

Promise 2: Avoidance of the "Second Death" (Smyrna)

> "Be faithful, even to the point of death, and I will give you life as your victor's crown. Whoever has ears, let them hear what the Spirit says to the churches. The one who is victorious will not be hurt at all by the second death." Revelation 2:10-11 (NIV)

There are options for how to think about this promise. I will briefly outline two approaches. Many believe the "second death" concerns life beyond this life. The scriptures tell us that *"people are destined to die once, and after that to face judgment"* (Hebrews 9:27, NIV). The Bible is clear that we have both a body and a spirit - an inner man and an outer man.[71] Our spirit is what lasts forever. Our love for God and the manifestation of this love in our actions is what transforms our spirit in this present life. We are called to "work out our salvation" so as to obtain a "better resurrection".[72] Just as there is spiritual reward for our faith in this life, so will there be in the life beyond life. From this perspective, the "second death" is understood as hell. Christ promises the obedient will avoid hell. This is the more traditional interpretation of this passage.

While this viewpoint is plausible, I believe the "second death" need not refer to something that happens beyond this life. Although the imagery would appear to suggest so, the book of Revelation was not written with the

---

[71] e.g. Matthew 16:26, 2 Corinthians 4:16, et al.

[72] "Therefore, my dear friends, as you have always obeyed – not only in my presence, but now much more in my absence – continue to work out your salvation with fear and trembling, for it is God who works in you to will and to act in order to fulfill his good purpose." Philippians 2:12 (NIV)

See also Hebrews 11:35 and surrounding verses.

traditionalist views of heaven and hell in mind. It was a "revelation," an unveiling of events that were *already taking place*. The book itself states: *"The revelation from Jesus Christ, which God gave him to show his servants what must soon take place"* (Revelation 1:1, NIV). *Soon* implies imminence. So, what could be meant by the "second death?"

The scriptures teach that we already died once with Christ.[73] We are now a new humanity that embody the realities of the new creation. We have been "born again" of the Spirit into a new kind of existence that is characterized by God's presence and the mind of Christ. We have been made alive in the Spirit. The "second death" therefore refers to our physical death, when we leave the earthly plane of existence. This makes sense given the context of the verse. Martyrdom was a very likely possibility for those in Smyrna. God promises that physical death is spiritual victory. He will never leave us or forsake us, and this promise extends to the potentially terrifying moment when our physical body dies. This promise is designed to disarm our fear of death, which is a ploy of our spiritual enemies.[74] Physical death is only a beginning for those who are in Christ. In Him, the best is always yet to come.

Promise 3: Hidden Manna, a White Stone, and a New Name (Pergamum)

> "Whoever has ears, let them hear what the Spirit says to the churches. To the one who is victorious, I will give some of the hidden manna. I will also give that person a white stone with a new name written on it, known only to the one who receives it." Revelation 2:17-18 (NIV)

Manna is the food of angels that fell from heaven to feed the Israelites when they were wandering the wilderness. Christ is our new manna, our bread of life. "Hidden manna" is wisdom, revelation, and insight concerning life in the kingdom of God. Paul writes, *"In Christ are hidden all treasures of wisdom and knowledge"* (Colossians 2:3, NIV). As we overcome suffering, God unveils to our spiritual sight the glorious realities of His kingdom and teaches us how to

---

[73] See Romans 6:4-8, Colossians 2:20, Galatians 2:20, 2 Corinthians 5:14, et al.

[74] "Since the children have flesh and blood, he too shared in their humanity so that by his death he might break the power of him who holds the power of death – that is, the devil – and free those who all their lives were held in slavery by their fear of death." Hebrews 2:14-15 (NIV)

abide in these realities. He shares His world with us. I believe "hidden manna" refers to spiritual meanings and interpretations hidden behind literal meanings in the Bible. The written Word of God is infinitely complex. As we grow in Christ, He prepares our hearts and minds to receive and comprehend this complexity.

The "white stone" is purity, innocence, and freedom from demonic accusations and condemnations. It is for freedom that Christ has set us free and there is no longer any condemnation based on past, present, or future failures. God is love - He is not mad at humanity, nor will He ever be. In our spiritual freedom, He allows us to freely reap what we sow.

Names throughout the Bible carry symbolic and prophetic meaning. Christ gives all of His followers new names. Simon became Peter (the rock). Saul became Paul (little). Our new name is given to us privately by the Holy Spirit and speaks of our spiritual destiny. Quiet yourself and ask the Lord to reveal your new name to you.

Promise 4: Authority Over the Nations and the Morningstar (Thyatira)

> "To the one who is victorious and does my will to the end, I will give authority over the nations - that one will 'rule them with an iron scepter and will dash them to pieces like pottery' - just as I have received authority from my Father. I will also give that one the morning star." Revelation 2:26-28, cf. Psalm 2:9 (NIV)

God's anointed kings are called to rule and reign in the earthly realm alongside Him. As we have learned, this reign is a reign of love. God's "authority" is not some sort of self-absorbed power that we can leverage against others, but divine empowerment for works of service. The "scepter" of Christ is divine justice and righteousness.[75] To "dash to pieces like pottery" is to demolish spiritual strongholds with God's love and truth.

---

[75] "Your throne, O God, will last for ever and ever; a scepter of justice will be the scepter of your kingdom. You love righteousness and hate wickedness…" Psalms 45:7 (NIV)

The "morningstar" speaks of Christ's light, which streaks into our hearts to illuminate the kingdom of God. Peter says, *"the day of the Lord will dawn and the morningstar will rise in your hearts"* (2 Peter 1:19, NIV). Jesus Himself says that He is the bright morning star.[76] The morningstar is revelation concerning the kingdom of God, which is already present amongst us. It illuminates what God is currently doing and will do as the kingdom advances on earth.

Promise 5: White Robes and the Book of Life (Sardis)

> "Yet you have a few people in Sardis who have not soiled their clothes. They will walk with me, dressed in white, for they are worthy. The one who is victorious will, like them, be dressed in white. I will never blot out the name of that person from the book of life, but will acknowledge that name before my Father and his angels." Revelation 3:4-5 (NIV)

We are the pure and spotless Bride of Christ. We wear white robes that symbolize purity and righteousness. White robes speak of purity and a clean conscience. We have been set free from consciousness of sin and have been given the mind of Christ. The mind of Christ allows us to share in His way of thinking.

The "book of life" is a metaphorical tome that contains the names of those who have been granted eternal life by God. This promise fills us with hope that we are held safe in Christ arms, despite failures or stumbles. Our names are in heaven's Book of Life. In the heavenly realm, Christ actively intercedes for us so that we may be empowered to win our spiritual battles.[77] He is always for us and never against us. As we achieve victory, Christ "acknowledges" our name before the Father and angels. To acknowledge someone is to do more than just consider them. When we acknowledge

---

[76] "I, Jesus, have sent my angel to give you this testimony for the churches. I am the Root and the Offspring of David, and the bright Morning Star." Revelation 22:16 (NIV)

[77] "If God is for us, who can be against us? He who did not spare his own Son, but gave him up for us all – how will he not also, along with him, graciously give us all things? Who will bring any charge against those whom God has chosen? It is God who justifies. Who then is the one who condemns? No one. Christ Jesus who died – more than that, who was raised to life – is at the right hand of God and is also interceding for us. Who shall separate us from the love of Christ?" Romans 8:31-35 (NIV)

someone, we are honoring them. Christ promises that we will be *honored* by heaven for overcoming, in this life and the next.

Promise 6: Pillars in the Temple of God (Philadelphia)

> "I am coming soon. Hold on to what you have, so that no one will take your crown. The one who is victorious I will make a pillar in the temple of my God. Never again will they leave it. I will write on them the name of my God and the name of the city of my God, the new Jerusalem, which is coming down out of heaven from my God; and I will also write on them my new name." Revelation 3:11-12 (NIV)

Notice here the royalty theme present in these verses (i.e. "crown" and "victorious"). God promises that He will make His victorious kings "pillars" in the temple of God. As we have explored, we are the new temple of the living God, the new Jerusalem. This is not a temple in the sense of a building, but a global humanity that shares a common experience of God's Holy Spirit. The "pillars" of this temple are not stone columns, but leaders to whom God has given grace to instruct, support, and exalt the Body of Christ. Paul himself mentions in Galatians 2:9 that Peter, James and John were considered "pillars" of the early church in Jerusalem.

The implication is that God offers to overcomers special leadership roles in the Body of Christ. These roles are "special" in the sense that they directly impact the spiritual needs of Christ's people. It is not about earthly superiority or exaltation. God gives some men and women particular graces and gifts that are intended to specifically impact the Body of Christ.

I believe God releases these graces to us during spiritual battles. In spiritual battle, we learn our true authority in Christ and the fullness of what has already been made available to us in His kingdom. It is less about God arbitrarily assigning gifts and more about us uncovering the fullness of what is already present. This happens when the fire of spiritual battle burns away our impurities so that the gold of Christ's presence within us can truly shine.

What does this passage mean when it says the New Jerusalem is "coming down out of heaven?" The New Jerusalem is the manifestation of heaven's reality in our reality (remember the Lord's Prayer: "On earth as it is in heaven"). The New Jerusalem is not a floating city that gradually descends out of the sky and lands in the Middle East. The New Jerusalem's "coming down out of heaven" is the progressive spiritual purification of the Body of Christ. This purification and restoration (salvation!) is what predicates Christ's appearing. In order for "every eye to see" Jesus Christ, our spirits must be prepared accordingly. We are already in this process. Christ has given us the privilege of bearing His name. He is already present in and amongst the new humanity.[78] As we grow in our royal identity and continue to steward divine realities, God's manifest presence amongst us will increase and become a true light to the nations.

Promise 7: Reign with Christ (Laodicea)

> "Here I am! I stand at the door and knock. If anyone hears my voice and opens the door, I will come in and eat with that person, and they with me. To the one who is victorious, I will give the right to sit with me on my throne, just as I was victorious and sat down with my Father on his throne." Revelation 3:20-21 (NIV)

We have already spent a great deal of time discussing how God's anointed kings are called to rule and reign with Christ. With this promise, I have also included the verse that comes before it because it is related to us reigning with Jesus. The "voice" of Christ is the Holy Spirit. The "door" is the human heart and mind. To open the door is to invite Christ into our lives, not only as our Lord, but as our friend and brother. To "eat" with Christ is to enjoy the blessings that He enjoys as He reigns over and sustains the entire universe. We walk through life in partnership with Him. We do not lack anything for our spiritual journey. As we ask in faith and trust that we have received what we have asked for, it will manifest in our experience.[79]

***

---

[78] "Surely I am with you always, to the end of the age." Matthew 28:20 (NIV)

[79] "Therefore I tell you, whatever you ask for in prayer, believe that you have received it, and it will be yours." Mark 11:24 (NIV)

These seven promises from Revelation beautifully summarize the fruits of Christian suffering. Suffering isn't for nothing - it manifests the realities of God's realm in us and through us. Spiritual warfare and the suffering that inevitably accompanies it can be expected in our journey into God's heart. Without tension, there can be no spiritual growth.

When God's truth comes into contact with the forces of wickedness in the heavenly realms, there is bound to be a spiritual reaction. When this reaction is particularly strong, suffering is experienced in our reality. God cannot share His throne with idols and the evil spirits that worship them. Suffering can be painful, but as we hold fast to the Word of Truth and persevere, we will find lasting victory. As the Holy Spirit says, *"There may be weeping in the night, but rejoicing comes in the morning"* (Psalms 30:5, NIV).

God's anointed kings demolish entrenched spiritual thinking patterns by taking thoughts captive and making them obedient to the character and nature of Christ. As our strongholds dissolve, our spiritual enemies run and flee, having lost their place of refuge in our hearts and minds. As we suffer internally and externally for the sake of Christ, His kingdom is realized within us and manifested through us. Like a mother in the pain of childbirth, our temporary suffering for the kingdom will result in indescribable glory.

Chapter Eleven

Judgment Day

Judgment is a loaded term in today's religious circles. When we hear it, it is easy to imagine a courtroom scene from a John Grisham book or movie. In these scenes, there is usually a morose judge who towers over the jury, prosecution, and defense. He quietly muses over the information presented to him before deciding on a final sentence. Eventually, the gavel falls, and a life-altering proclamation issues forth.

Modern Christianity has taken this idea and has applied it to the way we view God's "judgment." We are the defense, Jesus is our attorney, Satan and his demons are the prosecution, and the Father is the aloof judge. We believe that Jesus "interceding" for us means He is pleading our case before the Father so that we can avoid punishment and the fires of hell. Meanwhile, Satan and his minions sling vile accusations concerning our sinful deeds in the past and present. The Father then processes all this information and arrives at a judgment. We hope that Jesus has done enough to swing the Father's verdict in our favor.

In this incorrect yet incredibly prevalent conception of divine justice, God becomes an unstable schizophrenic - the Father and Jesus have two separate and distinct characters. The Father is out for blood, ready to punish anyone who stands in His way. Meanwhile, Jesus earnestly pleads with God for salvation on our behalf, reminding the Father that He went to the cross on our behalf to satisfy the divine bloodlust. Luckily for us, this satisfies the Father's pent-up wrath. The resurrected Son then gives to us a golden ticket that allows us to enter heaven when we die. This ticket is known as "imputed righteousness." Without this ticket, we remain as sinners subject to God's wrath in this life and hellfire in the beyond.

I am using hyperbole to make a point but many of us will realize that this is how we have been taught to subconsciously think about God. We consider Jesus and the Father to have different divine characteristics and functions. We view the Father as a divine spirit who is beyond the grasp of any mortal. We know that He loves us, but our mind often experiences this love as aloof, conditional, and temperamental. Jesus, however, loves us like crazy. He sits next to the Father and whispers in His ear the reasons why we shouldn't be punished for all of our sins. Jesus then sends the "advocate" of the heavenly courtroom, the Holy Spirit, to convict us of sin or make us feel an oh-so-rare touch of the Father's love. All of this is entirely dependent on our proper "Christian" behavior.

It would take a book to expose the fallacies of this line of thinking. What will suffice for our discussion is to understand that Jesus, as the "image" of the invisible God, *is* the most perfect representation of the Father. *In Christ, all of the fullness of the deity dwells in bodily form* (Colossians 2:9, NIV). This means that both the Father and the Holy Spirit are within Christ, and He is within them. They do not have three distinct personalities, attitudes, or "functions." Jesus said, "*I am in the Father, and the Father is in me*" (John 14:9) and, "*Whoever sees me sees the Once who sent me*" (John 12:45), and "*I and the Father are one*" (John 10:30). Therefore, God is love, joy, peace, patience, kindness, goodness, gentleness, faithfulness and self-control. The Bible is clear that He does not desire any to perish, but for all to come into a relationship with Him.[80] In light of this and the reality of the new creation, how are we to understand God's judgment? What role do God's anointed kings play in this judgment, if any?

---

[80] "The Lord is not slow in keeping his promise, as some understand slowness. Instead he is patient with you, not wanting anyone to perish, but everyone to come to repentance." 2 Peter 3:9 (NIV)

"Say to them, 'As surely as I live, declares the Sovereign Lord, I take no pleasure in the death of the wicked, but rather that they turn from their ways and live. Turn! Turn from your evil ways! Why will you die, people of Israel?'" Ezekiel 33:11 (NIV)

The Cross is the Judgment

Jesus Christ, in whom all the fullness of the deity dwells, reveals a God who is pure love. The cross is, above all, a powerful revelation of the true nature of the Father. Our understanding of anything in the Bible, no matter how it may present itself to our natural understanding, must be framed through the lens of Christ's love. The cross reveals a shocking truth: love is God's judgment.

> "For God so loved the world that he gave his only begotten Son, that whoever believes in him shall not perish but have eternal life. For God did not send his Son into the world to condemn the world, but to save the world through him." John 3:16-17 (NIV)

The cross was a once-for-all judgment not on humanity, but on the sin of the old creation order and the spiritual forces who empowered this sin. Paul writes: *"God made him who had no sin to be sin for us, so that in him we might become the righteousness of God"* (2 Corinthians 5:21, NIV). Christ's life was a rescue mission planned by the Father before time began. Jesus Christ was not a response to humanity's sin - He was God's plan all along. The lamb was slain before the foundation of the world![81] When the time was just right, when humanity was fully prepared to receive Him, God came in the flesh to save us, restore us, and inaugurate His kingdom on earth.

The legal (Old Testament) condemnation that haunted humanity as a consequence for sin was assumed by God on the cross. There is now no condemnation for those who are in Christ Jesus because the Holy Spirit has set us free from the old creation order and has brought us into the new.[82] The Holy Spirit is the agent who propels us into the fullness of the new creation. The old creation order in and around us - full of sin, death, and decay - has already begun to pass away.

---

[81] "All inhabitants of the earth will worship the beast – all whose names have not been written in the Lamb's book of life, the Lamb who was slain from the creation of the world." Revelation 13:8 (NIV)

[82] "Therefore, there is now no condemnation for those who are in Christ Jesus, because through Christ Jesus the law of the Spirit who gives life has set you free from the law of sin and death." Romans 8:1-2 (NIV)

"For he has rescued us from the dominion of darkness and brought us into the kingdom of the Son he loves…" Colossians 1:13 (NIV)

> "This world in its present form is passing away." 1 Corinthians 7:31 (**NIV**)
>
> "The world and its desires pass away, but whoever does the will of God lives forever." 1 John 2:17 (**NIV**)
>
> "For you have been born again, not of perishable seed, but of imperishable, through the living and enduring word of God. For, 'All people are like grass, and all their glory is like the flowers of the field; the grass withers and the flowers fall, but the word of the Lord endures forever.' And this is the word that was preached to you." 1 Peter 1:23-25 (**NIV**)
>
> "The night (the old creation order) is nearly over; the day (the fullness of the new creation) is almost here. So let us put aside the deeds of darkness and put on the armor of light." Romans 13:12 (**NIV**), parenthetical annotations mine

This entire book is about how we play a role in God's mission. God's anointed children hasten the Day of the Lord, which is the fullness of the kingdom of God, the era when everything in existence will once again align with its divine blueprint. The Body of Christ, empowered by the Holy Spirit, is the forerunner of this "Day."

How does God's wrath fit into this schema? The scriptures clearly tell us that those who do not place their trust in Christ remain under God's wrath.[83] God's wrath must be understood in light of His love, for He cannot deny Himself or violate His essential essence. God does not "punish" or "pour out wrath," as if He were an angry and unstable earthly father who needs to vent his rage on disobedient children. Wrath is the result of sin - it is what happens to us if we live out of accordance with the divine design. People willfully choose wrath by rejecting God's goodness and truth. Our decisions have consequences. We bear the spiritual fruit of deeds done in the body. Sin leads to death - in this life and the next. Sin's consequences are God's "wrath."

---

[83] "Whoever believes in the Son has eternal life, but whoever rejects the Son will not see life, for God's wrath remains on them." John 3:36 (NIV)

Think about it like this: Jesus currently upholds and sustains the universe with His love and power. This love and power operate according to the divine design, which never changes. *Jesus Christ is the same yesterday, today, and forever* (Hebrews 13:6, NIV). If we willfully choose to act out of line with the divine design, consequences result. There are immutable spiritual laws that we are not to transgress. If we do, we will experience the negative effects of our choices.

We live between two ages - the old and the new. The old creation order is currently subject to the wrath of God. The New Testament makes it clear that the wrath of God exists along three timelines - it had come, is already present, and will come. With this in mind, the proverbial "Day of Wrath" may not be an imminent, time-ending apocalyptic event, but an ongoing outpouring of God's wrath on everything and anything that belongs to the old creation order. False beliefs and evil behaviors must be burned away to make way for the new. God is creating streams of eternal life in the desert of humanity's brokenness and depravity.[84]

Paul writes, *"the wrath of God is being revealed from heaven against all godlessness and wickedness of people, who suppress the truth by their wickedness"* (Romans 1:18, NIV). This wrath manifests in human experience as depraved thinking, calamity, sickness, and all sorts of evil behavior that stand in opposition to God and His kingdom. Wrath shakes us awake to the reality of the new creation and God's kingdom. It is discipline, for God disciplines those He loves. God loves everything He has created, as John 3:16 reveals. The old creation humanity, with its darkened thought paradigms and wicked behaviors, now stands immersed in the fiery flames of God's purifying love.

A Consuming Fire

As God's wrath blazes against ungodliness, the kingdom advances like a raging fire. This fire will consume everything that is not of the character and nature of Jesus Christ. Peter writes about this fire in his Second Epistle:

---

[84] "Forget the former things; do not dwell on the past. See, I am doing a new thing! Now it springs up; do you not perceive it? I am making a way in the wilderness and streams in the wasteland." Isaiah 43:18-19 (NIV)

> "But the day of the Lord (the consummation of the kingdom) will come like a thief. The heavens will disappear with a roar; the elements will be destroyed with fire, and the earth and everything done in it will be burned up. Since everything will be destroyed in this way, what kind of people ought you to be? You ought to live holy and godly lives as you look forward to the day of God and speed its coming. That day will bring about the destruction of the heavens by fire, and the elements will melt in the heat. But in keeping with his promise we are looking forward to a new heaven and a new earth, where righteousness dwells." 2 Peter 3:10-13 (NIV), parenthetical annotations mine

This passage is often interpreted and understood rather literally, which is unfortunate. When approached in this manner, Peter's words appear to describe apocalyptic, universe-ending cosmic events. However, these verses allude to numerous Old Testament passages that speak of God fulfilling His promises to bring restoration, peace, and justice to the earth. In this passage, Peter has borrowed metaphoric language from the Hebrew prophets to paint a picture of humanity's spiritual destiny. He may have had in mind the following passages:

> "But who can endure the day of his coming? Who can stand when he appears? For he will be like a refiner's fire or a launderer's soap. He will sit as a refiner and purifier of silver; he will purify the Levites and refine them like gold and silver. Then the Lord will have men who bring offerings in righteousness." Malachi 3:2-4 (NIV)

> "'Surely the day is coming; it will burn like a furnace. All the arrogant and every evildoer will be stubble, and the day that is coming will set them on fire,' says the Lord Almighty." Malachi 4:1 (NIV)

> "See, the Lord is coming with fire, and his chariots are like a whirlwind; he will bring down his anger with fury, and his rebuke with flames of fire. For with fire and with his sword the Lord will execute judgment on all people." Isaiah 66:15-16 (NIV)

> "See, I will create new heavens and a new earth (the new creation). The former things (the old creation order) will not be remembered, nor will they come to mind." Isaiah 65:17 (NIV), parenthetical annotations mine

Fire is a notable symbolic motif throughout the scriptures that is commonly associated with God's illuminating and purifying presence. It evokes judgment, but not in the sense of damnation and condemnation. God's justice is His fiery love. To be subjected to God's justice is to be overwhelmed by His fire. In this fire, sin and impurity cannot remain. As we discussed earlier, God's people will be the first to face the fullness of this purifying fire. Judgment on the old creation order begins within God's household.[85] God is purifying His temple and increasing our capacity for His manifest presence and the fullness of the new creation. What is experienced by the Body of Christ will one day be experienced by the entire world. Remember, as the "sons of humanity," we are God's living signs and symbols that point to the future of the human race.

As God's fire progressively purifies us and the world, we receive into the natural realm a spiritual kingdom that cannot be shaken. At present, the winds of divine change sweep through heaven and earth:

> "'Once more I will shake not only the earth but also the heavens.' The words 'once more' indicate the removing of what can be shaken - that is, created things - so that what cannot be shaken may remain. Therefore, since we are receiving a kingdom that cannot be shaken, let us be thankful, and so worship God acceptably with reverence

---

[85] "If you suffer as a Christian, do not be ashamed, but praise God that you bear that name. For it is time for judgment to begin with God's household; and if it begins with us, what will the outcome be for those who do not obey the gospel of God?" 1 Peter 4:17 (NIV)

and awe, for our 'God is a consuming fire.'" Hebrews 12:26-28 (NIV)

The wind of the Holy Spirit casts into the purifying fire of God what is dead, lifeless, and irrelevant in the new creation. We experience this acutely during our personal spiritual battles, when we can feel the fire of God burning away what no longer has a place within us as new creations. John the Baptist promised that Jesus would baptize believers with the Holy Spirit and fire.[86] This fire is God's wrath and judgment being poured out upon our spiritual enemies. It purifies us so that we may receive, realize, and build the kingdom.

Joel's Army

So, what does any of this have to do with God's anointed new humanity? As God's kings in the new creation, we are responsible for partnering with the Lord in the administration of His judgment. His judgment is His justice. His justice is His love:

> "I will betroth thee unto me forever; yea, I will betroth thee unto me in righteousness, and in judgment, and in love, and in mercies." Hosea 2:19 (KJV)

> "For to us a child is born, to us a son is given, and the government will be on his shoulders. And he will be called Wonderful Counselor, Mighty God, Everlasting Father, Prince of Peace. Of the greatness of his government and peace there will be no end. He will reign on David's throne and over his kingdom, establishing and upholding it with justice and righteousness..." Isaiah 9:6-7 (NIV)

Along with the angels, we are responsible for releasing the pure fire of God's love:

---

[86] "I (John the Baptist) baptize you with water for repentance. But after me comes one who is more powerful than I, whose sandals I am not worthy to carry. He will baptize you with the Holy Spirit and fire." Matthew 3:11 (NIV)

> "He makes angels His messengers, His ministers flames of fire." Psalm 104:4 (NASB)

We currently sit in judgment on the old creation order alongside Christ. This means that we embody the good news of the new creation. We are ministers of reconciliation. Paul tells the Corinthians that believers will judge both the world and angels.[87] With the Holy Spirit, we administer God's justice through loving deeds that honor God and humanity. Speaking God's truth in love, we wage war against the evil principalities and powers that still hold sway over humanity.

> "In that day the Lord Almighty will be a glorious crown, a beautiful wreath for the remnant of his people. He will be a spirit of justice to the one who sits in judgment, a source of strength to those who turn back the battle at the gate." Isaiah 25:5-6 (NIV)

In the passage above, Isaiah mentions a "glorious crown." The mind of Christ is our glorious crown. The "spirit of justice" is the Holy Spirit that guides us in our role as God's anointed judges. It is clear from these verses in Isaiah that Christ supplies us with strength for our spiritual battles. Elsewhere, Isaiah speaks of the Body of Christ as mighty warriors who carry out the wrath of God:

> "Raise a banner on a bare hilltop, shout to them; beckon to them to enter the gates of the nobles. I have commanded those I prepared for battle; **I have summoned my warriors to carry out my wrath - those who rejoice in my triumph**. Listen, a noise on the mountains, like that of a great multitude! Listen, an uproar among the kingdoms, like nations massing together! The Lord Almighty is mustering an army for war. They come from faraway lands, from the ends of the heavens - the Lord and the weapons of his wrath - to destroy the whole country.

---

[87] "Do you not know that the Lord's people will judge the world? And if you are to judge the world, are you not competent to judge trivial cases? Do you not know that we will judge angels?" 1 Corinthians 6:2-3 (NIV)

Wail, for the day of the Lord is near; it will come like destruction for the Almighty." Isaiah 13:2-6 (NIV)

In a similar manner, the prophet Joel speaks of a "mighty army" that will sweep across the land on the Day of the Lord. This army is led by none other than Jesus Christ Himself:

> "Blow the trumpet in Zion; sound the alarm on my holy hill. Let all who live in the land tremble, for **the day of the Lord is coming. It is close at hand...a large and mighty army comes, such as never was in ancient times nor will ever be in ages to come. Before them fire devours, behind them a flame blazes**...Before them the earth shakes, the heavens tremble, the sun and moon are darkened, and the stars no longer shine. The Lord thunders at the head of his army; his forces are beyond number, and mighty is the army that obeys his command..." Joel 2:1-11 (NIV)

God's anointed kings are the army Joel describes. This army serves in total obedience, compelled by the Lord's mission to defeat His spiritual enemies and restore all of creation to its divine blueprint. Joel writes that this army *"does not jostle each other; each march straight ahead"* (2:8). This means the Lord has created for each anointed king unique works to walk in that will advance the kingdom. As we walk in these works, the "earth shakes and the heavens tremble." This is symbolic language that represents dramatic spiritual upheaval and subsequent manifestation in the natural realm (Peter does the same thing in 2 Peter 3:10-13, discussed above). Joel speaks of the kingdom of heaven.

Just as individuals are called into spiritual warfare, so is the corporate Body of Christ. Cultural spiritual strongholds such as abortion, sexual perversion, human trafficking, genocide, and pornography are all tangible manifestations of hell's kingdom. The forces of wickedness empowering issues are energized and fed by humanity's collective spiritual ignorance and rebellion from God. The more humanity willfully agrees with spiritual lies, the more powerful they become. The cultural strongholds that we see manifest today did not appear overnight. They were built lie upon lie, day by day, month by month, year by year. What we see in full bloom today is a spiritual regression and dissipation that has gone on for centuries. No single person is to blame for these problems and no single person can fix them. As a global family, we must learn how to address them together.

Cultural strongholds are a serious spiritual issue because they tear apart society from the inside out. This is evident from studying history. The spiritual health of a nation determines its future. When morality fragments, nations come unglued. Anyone can make evil appear as good by presenting it in a light that appears righteous to earthly sensibilities. In the end, evil is evil. We can paint over black mold and forget about it. This won't change the fact it will eventually make us all deathly sick like some insidious cancer.

Humanity as a whole is largely blind to the long-term consequences of our morality because we do not live with vision for the future. We live for ourselves. We are fixed on what is seen and focused on immediate gratification. What is most important to us is what we as individuals need in the moment, not what the collective may need hundreds of years from now. This is why we have no problem dropping atomic bombs and tearing the Earth apart.

The specter of all of our issues is absolutely enormous. If we focus on the problems, it is easy to become filled with hopelessness and apathy. In the face of such towering issues, what change can we truly make? This is why we as the Church must awaken to the fullness of our identity in Christ. We cannot keep doing the same thing over and over again and expect some sort of worldwide revival or awakening. What needs to change is the way we *think* about the gospel.

The restoration of the entire universe begins on the individual level. It begins with you and me awakening to the truth of who we are in Christ. If Jesus changed the entire creation order with just twelve men, what could happen with three billion Christians? *"All of creation groans waiting for the unveiling of the children of God,"* Paul writes in Romans 8:19. The groans of creation are earthquakes, tornadoes, hurricanes, floods, wars, and famines. All of these are the earth's tangible response to humanity's sin and spiritual ignorance. As we administer God's justice and humanity awakens to the reality of Christ's love, all of creation will respond accordingly:

> "My word that goes out from my mouth will not return to me empty, but will accomplish what I desire and achieve the purpose for which I sent it. You will go out in joy and be led forth in peace; the mountains and hills will burst into song before you, and all the trees of the field will clap their hands. Instead of the thornbush will grow the juniper, and instead of briers the myrtle will grow. This will be for the Lord's renown, for an everlasting sign, that will endure forever." Isaiah 55:11-13 (NIV)

Hellish strongholds do not appear in a day, and neither does the kingdom of God. Jesus said, *"The kingdom of God is like a man who scatters seed on the ground. Night and day, whether he sleeps or gets up, the seed sprouts and grows, though he does not know how. All by itself the soil produces grain - first the stalk, then the head, then the full kernel in the head. As soon as the grain is ripe, he puts the sickle to it, because the harvest has come"* (Mark 4:26-29, NIV).

The kingdom of God on earth grows slowly but surely as we steward divine realities in relationship with God and each other. Collective power in the kingdom rises as individuals unite together in spiritual effort. Cultural strongholds will fall as Christian communities bind together and overcome with Christ's love and truth. Corporate effectiveness requires individual process, conviction, passion, and obedience.

***

The ultimate truth is that Jesus did not come into the world to condemn the world, but to rescue and redeem it from sin's infection. The cross is the judgment on sin and death. By acting as a sin offering in humanity's stead, Christ disarmed the spiritual forces of sin and death that had oppressed us.

God currently pours out His wrath on all ungodliness and anything that stands in opposition to the truth of the new creation. This wrath is the consuming fire of God's love. Everything that belongs to the old creation order is subject to burn. We must understand that this wrath is not targeted at humanity, for God loves all and wishes for all to come into relationship with Him. Rather, it is our spiritual enemies that are subject to this devastating fury. Christ will fight for humanity in this way until our last spiritual enemy, death itself, is destroyed.[88]

God's anointed kings partner with Christ in the administration of His justice. We do this by binding together as one global family in order to confront and tear down societal spiritual strongholds. We wage war against these strongholds and the spiritual authorities that empower them by speaking the truth and relying on the guidance and direction of the Holy Spirit. As we do this, opposition and suffering may ensue, but we have the promise that our courage will not be in vain.

The fullness of the kingdom of heaven does not come about in a day. Before it is manifested externally, it must be realized internally. Christ empowers each of us to change the world in our own unique way. As we awaken to this reality, we step into the fullness of our divine calling. As we walk in the good works God has prepared for us and confront the principalities and powers with God's justice, we will hasten the Day of the Lord, the full consummation of the kingdom of heaven.

---

[88] "For he must reign until he has put all his enemies under his feet. The last enemy to be destroyed is death." 1 Corinthians 15:25-26 (NIV)

Chapter 12

The Shape of Things to Come

We have come to the end of our exploration of the spiritual offices of prophet, priest, and king. To succinctly summarize:

A **prophet** is an anointed individual who carries, identifies with, and releases the presence of Jesus Christ.

A **priest** is an anointed individual who offers spiritual sacrifices to God through worship, fellowship, and evangelism.

A **king** is an anointed individual who shares in the current rule and reign of Jesus Christ, wages spiritual warfare, and judges the world.

Through the anointing of the Holy Spirit, all believers are called to operate in these three offices. As we do, the kingdom of God is made manifest on earth and we progress into the fullness of Christ's victory on the cross.

A great deal of mind-bending biblical information has been presented, but many will find themselves asking the question: *What now?* After all, we are a people who rely on programs, formulas, and step-by-step instructions to get us where we need to be.

The answer is simple: *believe the message*. Everything else unfolds naturally after this. When we believe, God immediately begins speaking to us about our role in the new creation and the practical steps we can take to grow as individuals. We instantly become zealous for the greater things of the Lord. The message stokes a fire that the Holy Spirit fans into flame. Once ablaze, the fire remains so long as we continue to partner with the ascended Christ in the advancement of His kingdom.

New Creation Spirituality is not a discipleship program or a Christian self-help book. It is a new way of thinking. If we can think differently, we can begin to act differently. Many Christians today cry out for "revival" and "awakening" but are unwilling to change the way they think about the kingdom of God. Many of our existing ideas about God are actually what holds us back. We are like old computers that are unable to handle the latest and greatest programs. We want to run powerful new software but are unwilling to change our operating system. New wine cannot be poured into old wineskins.

It is fear that causes us to cling to what is known and familiar. So long as there is fear, we can never have "revival" or "awakening." Fear is the kingdom of God's greatest opponent. It opposes the fresh work of the Holy Spirit and breeds sin, division, and religionism.

The greatest challenge of our time does not come from without, but from within. We must be willing to surrender our antiquated understandings, lifeless rituals, and entrenched beliefs for the possibility of something far greater. Only then will we be able move into the future with vision, confidence, and power.

The End is Near?

Our postmodern era is rife with spiritual challenges. It is a temptation to view the times as the darkest ever, but if we strive to look from heaven's point of view, we will see that this simply cannot be true. Two thousand years ago, a great light dawned in mankind's spiritual history. This light was embodied in the person of Jesus Christ, who began His ministry by calling twelve followers to obedience. Thousands of years later, billions of people believe His message and call on His name.

Fearful religionists would have us believe that we are headed to hell in a handbasket. To them, the evidence is conclusive: modern society is doomed to imminent destruction. Jesus will soon ride in on a cloud in the earth's atmosphere to put believers out of their misery by taking them to heaven. Sinners, those who have not made an intellectual assent to Christian doctrine, will be thrown into the everlasting fires of hell.

The ignorance of this position is made more appalling by the fact that this is what the majority of Christians believe and actively profess as the gospel. It's no wonder an unbelieving world has such a hard time with the Christian faith. Of course there will be resentment about an intellectual message that excludes billions of people! The entire point of this book has been to call into question the predominating Christian message by shedding light on a first-century understanding of Christ's gospel.

As has been hopefully made clear at this point, the gospel is not an intellectual message that must be received in order to "get to heaven." Post-life spiritual existence was not the main focus of the apostles and the early church. Yes, there will be a resurrection of the dead and a final judgment, but any details beyond this are surprisingly unclear in the Bible. Most of what we have been taught to believe about heaven and hell is a dubious mix of theology and American folk religion.

We know that there is spiritual reward - we will certainly bear the everlasting fruit of our activities on earth. But what was most important to the earliest apostles must be our focus: Jesus died and rose again, initiating a new creation order. We are called to respond in loving obedience. The Holy Spirit now empowers us to live as a new humanity that properly belongs in this new creation order. If we do die, God will eventually raise us from the dead. There will be a final "interview" with Christ, in which we will give an account for the deeds done in the body.[89] The sons of God now steward these realities and live accordingly to advance the kingdom.

The first-century gospel was a declared revelation that Christ had come to save humanity from the spiritual forces of darkness that oppressed us:

---

[89] "For we must all appear before the judgment seat of Christ, so that each of us may receive what is due us for the things done while in the body, whether good or bad." 2 Corinthians 5:10 (NIV)

"People are destined to die once, and after that to face judgment..." Hebrews 9:27 (NIV)

> "He has saved (rescued) us and called us to a holy (set apart) life - not because of anything we have done (religious works) but because of his own purpose and grace (the initiation of the new creation). This grace (which is access to God's presence) was given us in Christ Jesus before the beginning of time, but it has now been revealed through the appearing of our Savior, Christ Jesus, who has destroyed death and has brought life and immortality (both current, ever-increasing realities) to light through the good news (which is the Word of God, embodied in Christ)." 2 Timothy 1:9-10 (NIV), parenthetical annotations mine

To accomplish this incredible feat, Christ acted as a once-for-all sacrifice that freed human consciousness from the shackles of religion, sin, and darkness. His death and resurrection was a judgment on the old creation order, an order that is currently in the process of passing away. He has given us the Holy Spirit, who allows us to live victoriously in between the initiation and consummation of His kingdom. As we mature in our personal and corporate identity as the bride of Christ, the kingdom is made manifest. Now is the time of God's favor, now is the day of salvation!

So, what about the concept of the "last times?" What about all of the doom and gloom that seems to dominate modern religious thinking? Are the times as dark as the fear-mongering establishment would have us believe? I wholeheartedly believe the answer is *no*.

Today more than ever, people have access to the Word of Truth. Most have at least heard the name of Jesus. The faith is exploding around the world, especially in underdeveloped nations and third-world countries. For two thousand years, the gospel has been unstoppable. It is the power of God for those who believe. Like a grand tree, the salvation of the globe is developing and rising upward day by day, slowly but surely. So much fruit has already been harvested, and so much more is to come.

But what about the proverbial "last days?" How should we understand them in light of the new creation and the current reality of God's kingdom? What did the apostles have in mind when they wrote on the "last days?"

> "But mark this: There will be terrible times in the last days. People will be lovers of themselves, lovers of money, boastful, proud, abusive, disobedient to their parents, ungrateful, unholy, without love, unforgiving, slanderous, without self-control, brutal, not lovers of the good, treacherous, rash, conceited, lovers of pleasure rather than lovers of God - having a form of godliness but denying its power. Have nothing to do with such people." 2 Timothy 3:1-5 (NIV)

It is a mistake to believe that these words were somehow exclusively intended for our modern age. In this passage, Paul describes to Timothy the characteristics of the age of the old-world order that is already in the process of passing away. These words are *timeless* - they apply to an unbelieving society until the consummation of the fullness of the kingdom of heaven, when the knowledge of God's glory covers the entire earth.

In the passage above, Paul's words to Timothy are less of a warning about some sort of impending anti-spiritual zeitgeist and more of a characterization of the current age.[90] The reality is that for two thousand years we have lived in the "end times." We live between two ages, the old and the new. In the meantime, God's kingdom advances, and faith-filled men and women around the world forcefully lay hold of it.

> "[Jesus] was chosen before the creation of the world, but was **revealed in these last times** for your sake. Through him you believe in God, who raised him from the dead and glorified him, and so your faith and hope are in God." 1 Peter 1:20 (NIV)

> "The world is passing away, and also its lusts; but the one who does the will of God lives forever. Children, **it is the last hour**..." 1 John 2:17-18 (NIV)

> "In the past God spoke to our ancestors through the prophets at many times and in various ways, **but in these**

---

[90] Peter does something similar in 2 Peter 3:2-7.

> **last days** he has spoken to us by his Son, whom he appointed heir of all things, and through whom also he made the universe." Hebrews 1:1-2 (NIV)

A great challenge exists today within the Body of Christ. The many divisions and arguments in the faith only serve to show how much sin currently exists in the corporate Body. We cannot be a true light in the world until we are healed and made whole - brought to fullness, unity and maturity.

Before the Body of Christ can save the world, it must allow itself to be saved. As we have learned, to be "saved" is to be fully restored and renewed into the image of Jesus Christ. In Christ, there are no divisions brought about by worldly thinking or intellectual idolatry. Knowledge puffs up but love and a mutual experience of God's presence builds up. As we mature in a corporate, experiential knowing of the son of God, the kingdom of heaven will manifest in greater and greater measure.

Honor Thy Father and Mother

There is certainly a tension in the corporate spiritual maturation process. This tension exists between the known and the unknown, between what is already understood and what is yet to be revealed. We know that the destiny of the Body of Christ is a "fullness," a "unity in the faith," and a "perfect" knowledge of Jesus Christ.[91] For now, we see and know God's fullness in part, but when the perfect knowledge of Jesus Christ comes, we shall know fully, just as we are fully known by Him.

> "For we know in part and we prophesy in part; but when the perfect comes, the partial will be done away...For now we see in a mirror dimly, but then face to face; now I know in part, but then I will know fully just as I also have been fully known." 1 Corinthians 13:9,12 (NASB)

---

[91] "So Christ himself gave the apostles, the prophets, the evangelists, the pastors and teachers, to equip his people for works of service, so that the body of Christ may be built up until we all reach unity in the faith and in the knowledge of the Son of God and become mature, attaining to the whole measure of the fullness of Christ." Ephesians 4:11-13 (NIV)

The "perfect" in this passage is not some sort of sudden, time-ending apocalyptic event, but the *culmination of spiritual maturity* in the Body of Christ. This is achieved through the work of prophets and apostles, who carefully build upon established understandings and revelations about the cross. The foundation of understanding, the cornerstone of all genuine revelation, is Jesus Christ and His life, death, and resurrection. For two thousand years, the Body has been growing in wisdom and stature, striving to attain to the whole fullness of what was accomplished by Jesus Christ.

A major stumbling block in the Body of Christ is the belief that we are meant to remain fixed in our understanding of the Messiah's work. Deep religious fears and intellectual idolatry have prevented us from moving forward in the faith. Because of this, stagnation and religionism hold sway. An intellectual faith has overshadowed an intuitive relationship with God. With an intellectual faith comes pride and legalistic thinking patterns. With pride and legalistic thinking patterns come sin. With sin comes eventual death. Our understanding of Jesus Christ's finished work must constantly grow and mature. If we don't grow, we perish.

A good analogy for this is a volcano that has just erupted. As lava flows down the side of the mountain, it destroys everything in its path. There is great power and transformation at the front of the lava flow. Fresh lava violently and dramatically re-shapes the landscape. Eventually, the lava will cool and harden. When it does, it no longer holds any sort of power to enact change in its environment. However, it can be approached, studied, and, therefore, understood according to the wisdom of man.

This is exactly how corporate revelation works. The eruption is the gospel of Christ. The front of the lava flow is the fresh, spontaneous work of the Holy Spirit, who reveals the fullness of the kingdom. The path of the lava is hard to discern, and no one is really sure where it is going.[92] It can be absolutely terrifying because it is spontaneous, uncontrollable, and unstoppable.

It is apostles and prophets who aim to live in step with this raw flow of power. When the lava hardens, it becomes religion and theology. Religionists prefer

---

[92] "The wind blows wherever it pleases. You hear its sound, but you cannot tell where it comes from or where it is going. So it is with everyone born of the Spirit." John 3:8 (NIV)

lava that is cooled and hardened because it is safe and contained. The problem is that we can mistake hardened lava for actual lava. It becomes our sole focus because we feel we can touch it, study it, and understand it. If we feel we can understand it, we gain a false sense of intellectual control over it. This is the essence of religionism.

Any careful student of the Bible will tell you that there is a developing revelation of the cross throughout the New Testament epistles. This is where the spotlight falls on Paul. Although an apostle of Christ, his convictions and revelation put him in conflict with the established Christian church in Jerusalem. His revelation of spiritual freedom often put him at odds with the other believers such as James and Peter, who still stressed some legalistic paradigms of Judaism.[93] At the end of the day, they were all still "Christians" in the sense that they enjoyed a vibrant relationship with the living Messiah. But, they had different revelations of the cross.

Revelation of the finished work of the cross continues to develop over time. God sends apostles and prophets to the Body in order to mature our understanding of what has already been accomplished. Apostles and prophets illuminate new dimensions of the gospel in order to combat the darkness of their respective ages. They bring revelation. This is where fear can creep in - how do we know what is from God and not from God? Isn't it easier to stay with what is known? Will we be deceived?

Genuine revelation is centered on Christ crucified and will not go beyond what is written in the scriptures. Deception often goes beyond what is written in order to appear unique and novel. We have some insight on this issue in the Bible. *"Honor your father and mother,"* the scriptures instruct us, *"that you may live long in the land the Lord your God is giving you"* (Exodus 20:12, NIV). Authentic revelation honors what has already been established by our forefathers in the faith (our "fathers" and "mothers"), and proceeds to build on this established revelation. By honoring what has come before, God promises to give spiritual life to what is fresh and forthcoming. A tree grows upward by the support of what is below.

---

[93] This conflict is documented in Galatians.

There will always be a tension between those who feel strongly about what has already been established and those who press onward into new understandings with faith and trust. There will always be "Pharisees" (those zealous for the establishment) and there will always be "Christs" (reformers and prophets who bring the new). Old meets new is always a formula for conflict and suffering. As a Body, we must embrace this tension with love for each other. There can be no growth without growing pains. The Father will work through this tension to bring forth what He desires for His people. *"Where two or three are gathered in my name, there I am among them,"* says the Lord (Matthew 18:20, NIV).

Fresh revelation is thrilling and exciting. For those blessed with revelatory gifts, it can be tempting to leave the flock and run onward into strange and unfamiliar spiritual territory. This is unwise. Prophets are subject to the authority of other prophets. Spiritual pioneers would do well to remember that the ultimate mandate is to love, and this means bearing with the Body of Christ in its current level of understanding and experience. Revelation must serve the way of love, which is the way of Christ. If one can fathom all mysteries and yet not love, they are nothing. Fresh revelation is a meal that must be served in the name of love. Without love, it is not digestible and therefore useless. Unless the Lord builds the understanding of His fullness precept upon precept and line upon line, revelation will be in vain.

New Perspectives

New creation spirituality encourages us to approach Christianity in a new light. It is about new perspectives, new angles and, most importantly, new priorities. Our ability to enact change as a God's anointed people is largely dependent on our ability to *think* as a new humanity. If we can think like Jesus, we will be naturally empowered to act like Him. We have the mind of Christ!

New creation thinking reorients the focus of our faith from the idyllic "beyond" to the raw reality of the present. Yes, life after life is important and obviously informs how we should live our lives here on earth, but it should never be the main focus of our faith. As Paul writes, we have been rescued from the dominion of darkness and brought into Christ's reign of light.[94] We do not lack vision and stumble around in darkness. Christ's light shines through our hearts and minds to illuminate the present. We are called to act powerfully in this present as God's anointed children. As we live in this faith, His light shines through us, bringing greater clarity to a plan for humanity that is already in motion.

A powerful truth resounds from Proverbs 29:18: *"Where there is no vision, the people cast off restraint."* What the faith desperately needs right now is a clear vision for the future, not nebulous wishful thinking. We need to re-evaluate the effectiveness and power of our current *modus operandi*. Ideas and actions that do not manifest the present reality of the kingdom of God must be done away with. It is no longer time for empty words and vain spiritual activity. The kingdom is a present, ever-increasing reality, and we must be willing to adjust our theology, thinking, and worship to accommodate it. If we do not, we will exclude ourselves from what God is doing on the earth.

We must seek a clearer vision of what the future holds. Spiritual vision is powerful. It draws believers and unbelievers alike because it radiates the faith, hope, and love of the kingdom of God. I believe it is something that all human beings crave. Vision brings focus, purpose, and determination to our lives. Without vision, we become stagnant in our spiritual journey and prone to the sin that so easily entangles us. Doing the same thing over and over again on Sunday morning and expecting some sort of unprecedented supernatural result is the very definition of insanity. We are the children of God, not religious slaves. God's mercies are new every morning. There is always a fresh wind of the Spirit available for us to flow in, but we must be willing to lay aside our fear and pride.

New creation spirituality encourages us to engage with what God is currently doing in and amongst His people. The Father is always at work, and we too must work. We do this though the power of the anointing, serving as prophets, priests, and kings in God's current reign of love. We must be wary of any teaching that emphasizes a delay in the kingdom of God and prioritizes the teachings of man. The Holy Spirit is present in the earth! We live on every

---

[94] "Give joyful thanks to the Father, who has qualified us to share in the inheritance of his holy people in the kingdom of light. For he has rescued us from the dominion of darkness and brought us into the kingdom of the Son he loves, in whom we have redemption, the forgiveness of sins." Colossians 1:12-14 (NIV)

word that proceeds from the mouth of God, which is the Holy Spirit. As Peter writes in 2 Peter 1:3, *"His divine power has given us everything we need for a godly life through our knowledge of him who called us by his own glory and goodness."* To rephrase what Peter is saying: God's gift of the anointing actively empowers us to live in an experience of God and His kingdom. Christian faith is not about what God is "going to do," but what God has done and is currently doing. No more delay. No more waiting. As we steward this reality, we hasten the "Day of the Lord," the consummation of the kingdom of God.

Vision requires us to broaden our narrow perspectives. Jesus Christ crucified is the turning point in the history of mankind. It is the starting point of an entirely new creation order. Our faith is not our own. We now join in with millions upon millions of other believers - past, present, and future. Together, as one family united in the Spirit, we strive to attain to the fullness of the gospel. We love together, we suffer together, and we will reign together. Nothing is wasted, and God promises to vindicate those who have fallen asleep in death.

Christianity was never supposed to be a Sunday morning antidepressant, but a global, history-spanning rescue mission. We must build on what has come before while anticipating what must come next. Our thinking about the gospel must extend beyond ourselves. Every contribution to the kingdom will reverberate throughout the centuries. With this in mind, our attitudes, words, and actions carry so much more weight. Our collective mission spans throughout history and covers the entire earth. With this perspective in mind, we are emboldened to take up the work left to us by the saints who have walked before us. We must be vigilant so not to lose what has already been accomplished for the sake of Jesus Christ.

> "Therefore, since we are surrounded by such a great cloud of witnesses, let us throw off everything that hinders and the sin that so easily entangles. And let us run with perseverance the race marked out for us, fixing our eyes on Jesus, the pioneer and perfecter of faith." Hebrews 12:1-2 (NIV)

Iron Sharpens Iron

The key to seeing the future is understanding the role of the present. If we can adopt a global, history-spanning perspective, we will begin to understand where God might be taking His people. First-century Christianity was birthed through a profound revelation of God's character and nature. The Messiah had come to rescue God's chosen people by fulfilling (embodying) the prophetic writings of the Hebrews. It was revealed, however, that this rescue mission would extend not only to the Jews, but to the entire world. The signifying mark of rescue and renewal (salvation) in God's new creation humanity was the dynamic presence of the Holy Spirit.

Over time, the flame began to die down. The lava that had once flowed freely became a hardened form that cast a pale shadow on the glory that had come before. What was once experiential and largely intuitive became rigid, intellectual, and institutionalized. A dynamic experience of the Holy Spirit's power faded into the realm of theory.

Doctrine, tradition, and institutionalized Christianity have served to faithfully preserve the faith throughout the centuries, but they cannot address the moral and spiritual needs of our current age. Where sin increases, grace, God's empowering presence, must increase.[95]

For hundreds of years, God has slowly but surely been breaking us out of our rigid intellectual faith paradigms and restoring us to the primitive spirituality of the first-century Jesus movement. This spirituality is oriented around God's presence and the spiritual offices of prophet, priest, and king.

Right now, it is obvious that there is an incredible tension in the Body between the intellectual faith and the intuitive faith. The intellectual faith relies heavily on teaching about doctrine, proper knowledge of God, and biblical instructions for godly living. The intuitive faith focuses more on the dynamic experience of the Holy Spirit, spiritual gifts, and personal revelation. Which emphasis is more correct? The answer, of course, is neither.

---

[95] "Where sin increased, grace increased all the more, so that, just as sin reigned in death, so also grace might reign through righteousness to bring eternal life through Jesus Christ our Lord." Romans 5:20-21 (NIV)

"*As iron sharpens iron, so one man sharpens another*" (Proverbs 27:17, NIV). The experiential and intellectual sides of faith grind against each other in the furnace of God's intentional long-term process. They sharpen and refine each other. We need correct knowledge of God to be able to encounter Him on an experiential level. For now, proper Christian teaching and doctrine serve as tutors that help us steward the spiritual liberty that comes with divine sonship. *Those led by the Spirit of God are the sons of God* (Romans 8:14). As we grow individually and corporately in this freedom, our ability to be led by the Spirit begins to supersede our need for doctrine and man-made theologies about God. We move from milk, basic teaching about God, to solid food, which is what the Father is speaking and saying to us in the moment. The promise of the prophets is that one day we will no longer need teachers, because we will all be perfectly led by the Father. This is the full glory of the New Covenant.

> "'This is the covenant I will establish with the people of Israel after that time', declares the Lord. 'I will put my law in their minds and write it on their hearts. I will be their God, and they will be my people. No longer will they teach their neighbor, or say to one another, 'Know the Lord,' because they will all know me, from the least of them to the greatest,' declares the Lord. 'For I will forgive their wickedness and will remember their sins no more.'"
> Jeremiah 31:33-34 (NIV)

I picture a spaceship that is preparing for an unprecedented launch. Imagine that this spaceship is the Body of Christ, space is the fullness of the kingdom of heaven, and the ship's fuel pods are intellectual knowledge about God. When the ship takes off, it requires an enormous amount of fuel. When it enters space, however, the fuel pods are ejected and fall back to Earth, having served their purpose. Having reached its destination, the spaceship is no longer in need of the fuel that was once so essential to its mission.

What I am not saying is that we no longer need the Bible or great scriptural teaching. That is absurd. The Lord is present in His Word. I am speaking to an issue. Our faith is heavily enmeshed in religionism and idolatrous worship of the Bible. We have become arrogant and ignorant in our coveting of spiritual knowledge. Knowledge puffs up, but love builds up. As we learn to experience God and His goodness, we gain a profound revelation of His love for us. It is this revelation that changes our behavior and increases our effectiveness as disciples of the kingdom of heaven. Knowledge must launch us into an experience of God's love. If it does not, it is utterly useless.

This process, this spiritual evolution in Christ's Body, will not occur overnight. It will take hundreds if not thousands of years for us to grow into our full maturity. As the Bride of Christ, we are growing in intimacy with our Husband. We are gaining a deeper understanding of His movements and learning how to join Him in His divine dance with humanity. We are slowly but surely moving into His fullest intention for our marriage.

God has appointed times and seasons for His purposes, and we must humble ourselves to abide in this reality. God is patient, wishing for all to come to a change of heart. With the Lord, a thousand years is like a day and a day is like a thousand years. This helps us understand that the "Day of the Lord" may not be an instantaneous *deux ex machina*, but a gradual process of purification, restoration, and renewal that will span many years. The culmination is a unity between God's realm (heaven) and our realm (earth) and the destruction of the last enemy, death. As Paul writes, *"He must reign until He has put all enemies under his feet. The last enemy to be destroyed is death"* (1 Corinthians 15:25-26, NIV). Let the prophets, priests, and kings serve with the Almighty until the fullness of His will is accomplished, on earth as it is in heaven.

Author's Note

I want to personally thank the reader for joining me in this adventure into God's heart. It is my hope that the truths presented in this book challenge you to think in new ways. A new way of thinking propels us into a new way of being. It is this wonderful new way of being that has power to transform the world.

I didn't write this book with a "blow-it-up-start-again" mindset. This book is for the Church. God's global family is destined to evolve in the safety of God's love. We are called to press onward. By actively walking with Christ, we grow into the fullness of His intentions. He is the Alpha and the Omega, the beginning and the end. "End" implies a final destination. This destination is the fiery center of God's heart.

I want to encourage you to talk with God about the content of this book. What do you agree and disagree with? Feel free to disagree. Ask Jesus for your next steps. He will be faithful to illuminate your individual path. As individuals are set aflame with love, purpose, and vision, our entire spiritual family begins to burn a little bit brighter. It is my prayer that a roaring fire soon covers the earth.

Yours in Christ,

Michael Reinemann

NOW AVAILABLE ON AMAZON

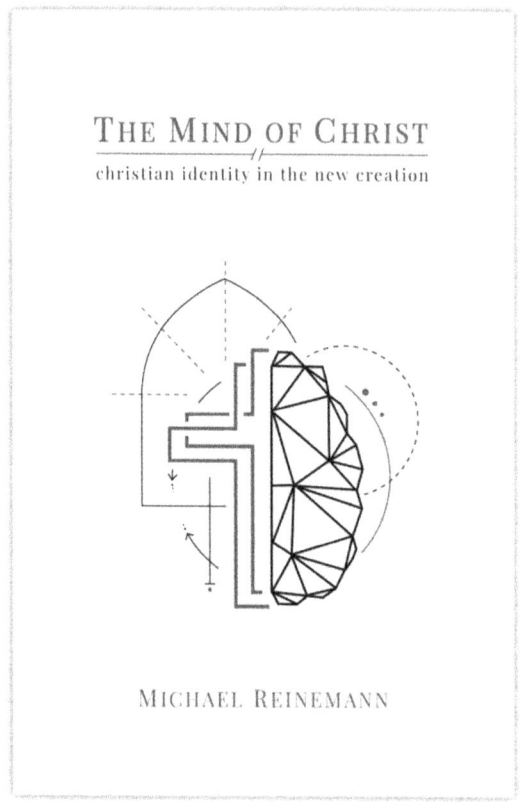

My first book, *The Mind of Christ: Christian Identity in the New Creation*, is now available in paperback or e-book on Amazon.com. *The Mind of Christ* explores Christian identity, the renewing of the mind, and spiritual gifts in light of the new creation. Using my personal testimony as a platform, I explore humanity's union with Christ and the supernatural fruits of this union. This book illuminates spiritual process and will awaken you to the fullness of God's supernatural purpose for your life. It will encourage and inspire you to walk in the fullness of your identity as a Christ-one and God's son or daughter.

For more on new creation realities, or to connect with the author, please visit:

www.seekingHismind.com

www.ingramcontent.com/pod-product-compliance
Lightning Source LLC
LaVergne TN
LVHW041616070426
835507LV00008B/285